Bootleg Country Guitar

100% Accurate

All The Best Twangy Tunes!

ISBN: 978-1-4950-6571-2

7777 W. BLUEMOUND RD. P.O. BOX 13819 MILWAUKEE, WI 53213

Visit Hal Leonard Online at
www.halleonard.com

RHYTHM TAB LEGEND

Rhythm Tab is a form of notation that adds rhythmic values to the traditional tab staff.

TABLATURE graphically represents the guitar fingerboard. Each horizontal line represents a string, and each number represents a fret. Rhythmic values are shown using ovals, stems, and dots.

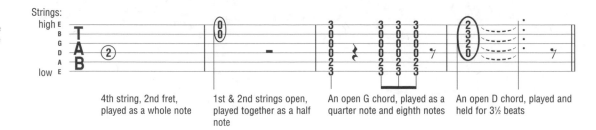

4th string, 2nd fret, played as a whole note

1st & 2nd strings open, played together as a half note

An open G chord, played as a quarter note and eighth notes

An open D chord, played and held for 3½ beats

Definitions for Special Guitar Notation

HALF-STEP BEND: Strike the note and bend up 1/2 step.

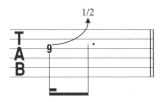

WHOLE-STEP BEND: Strike the note and bend up one step.

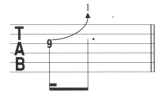

SLIGHT (MICROTONE) BEND: Strike the note and bend up 1/4 step.

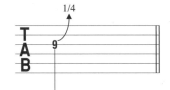

BEND AND RELEASE: Strike the note and bend up as indicated, then release back to the original note. Only the first note is struck.

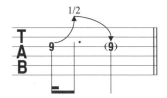

PRE-BEND: Bend the note as indicated, then strike it.

GRACE NOTE PRE-BEND AND RELEASE: Bend the note as indicated. Strike it and release the bend back to the original note.

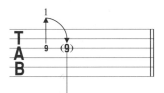

UNISON BEND: Strike the two notes simultaneously and bend the lower note up to the pitch of the higher.

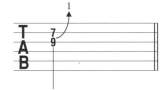

HOLD BEND: While sustaining bent note, strike note on different string.

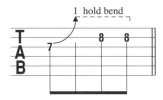

VIBRATO: The string is vibrated by rapidly bending and releasing the note with the fretting hand.

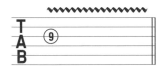

WIDE VIBRATO: The pitch is varied to a greater degree by vibrating with the fretting hand.

HAMMER-ON: Strike the first (lower) note with one finger, then sound the higher note (on the same string) with another finger by fretting it without picking.

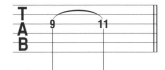

PULL-OFF: Place both fingers on the notes to be sounded. Strike the first note and without picking, pull the finger off to sound the second (lower) note.

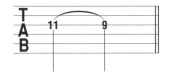

HAMMER FROM NOWHERE: Sound note(s) by hammering with fret hand finger only.

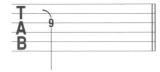

GRACE NOTE SLUR: Strike the note and immediately hammer-on (or pull-off) as indicated.

GRACE NOTE SLUR (CLUSTER): Strike the notes and immediately hammer-on (or pull-off) as indicated.

LEGATO SLIDE: Strike the first note and then slide the same fret-hand finger up or down to the second note. The second note is not struck.

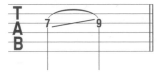

Ain't Goin' Down
('Til the Sun Comes Up)

Words and Music by Kim Williams, Garth Brooks and Kent Blazy

Guitar: Chris Leuzinger

Key of G

Intro

Fast

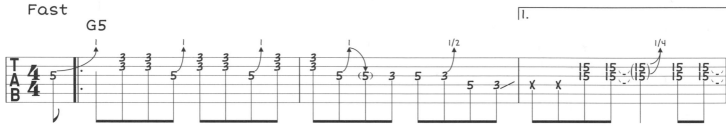

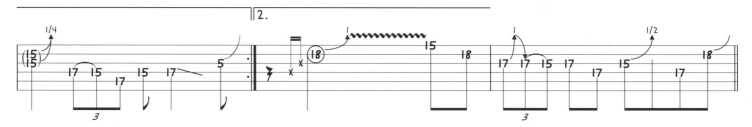

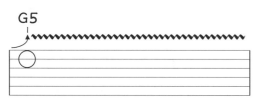

Verse

Six o' clock

	G5		G5		G5		G5		
	C5		C5		G5		G5		
	D5		D5		G5		G5	*F5		

*Include 1st time only.

Interlude

| |G5 | |G5 | |G5 | |G5 | || |

Chorus

They ain't goin' down

| | C | | C | | G | | G | B♭ | |
| | C | |²⁄₄ C | |⁴⁄₄ | | | | |

Harmonica Solo

|G5	|G5	|G5	|G5	
|C5	|C5	|G5	|G5	
|D5	|D5	|G5	|G5 F5	‖

Bridge

Ten 'til twelve

	G N.C.		G N.C.		C N.C.		G N.C.	
	D N.C.		D N.C.		G		G	‖

Interlude

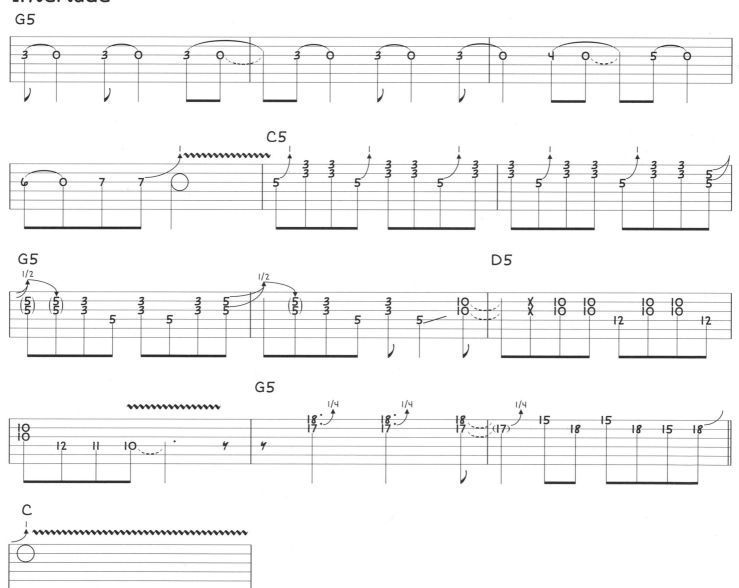

Verse

Six o'clock

|G5 |G5 |G5 |G5   C#5|

|D5 |D5 |G5 |G5 ||

Guitar Solo

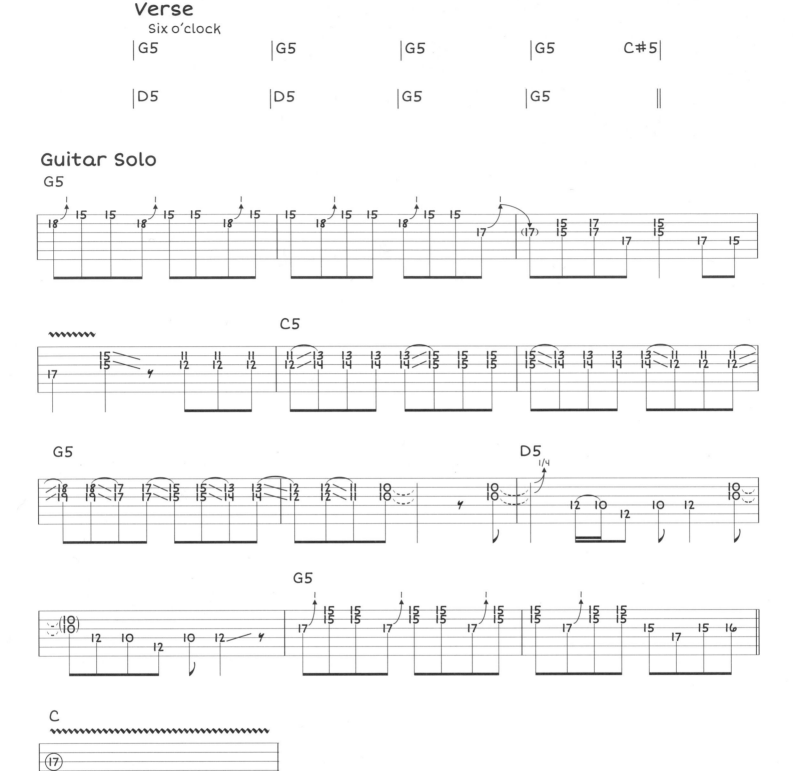

Outro-Solos

w/ Verse pattern

Cannon Ball Rag

By Merle Travis

Guitar: Merle Travis

Key of G

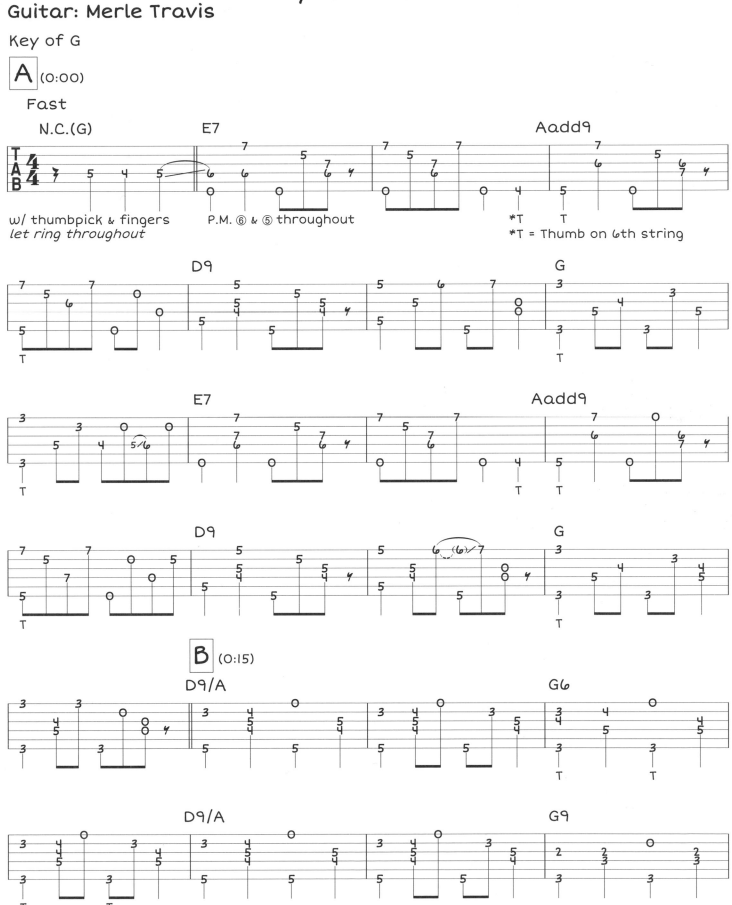

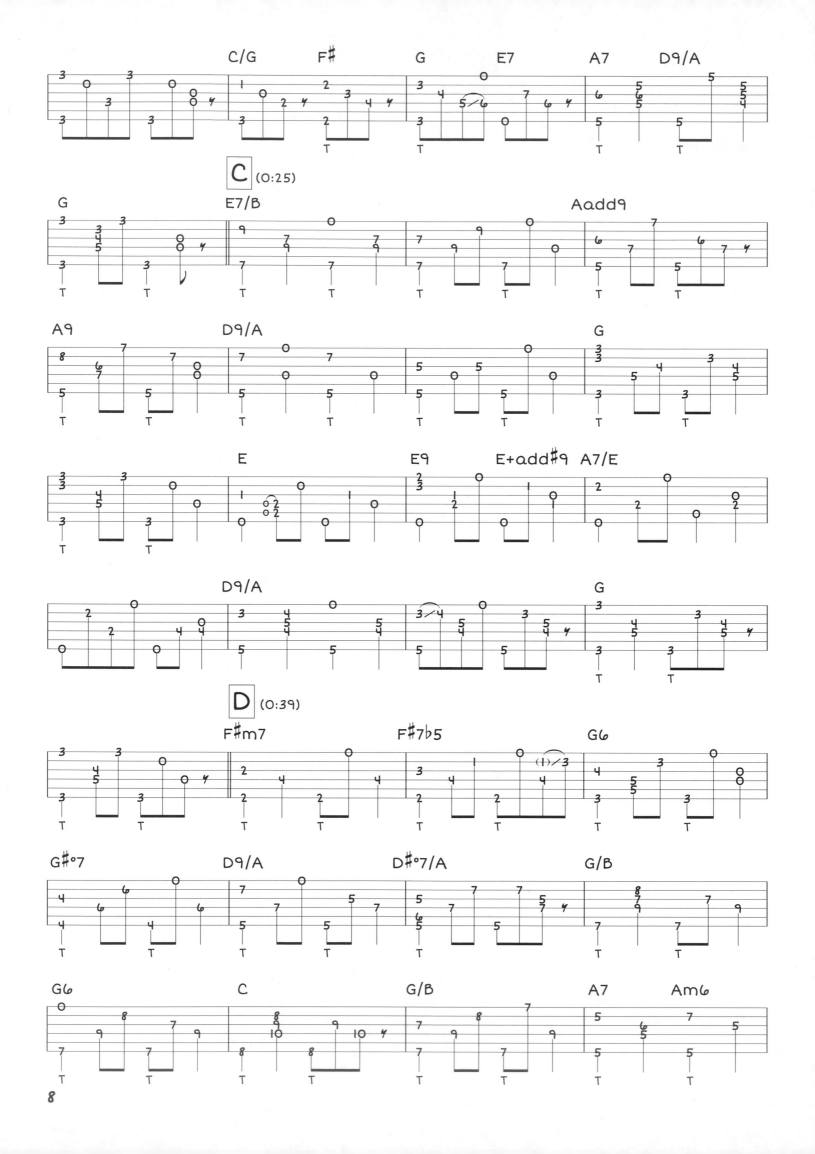

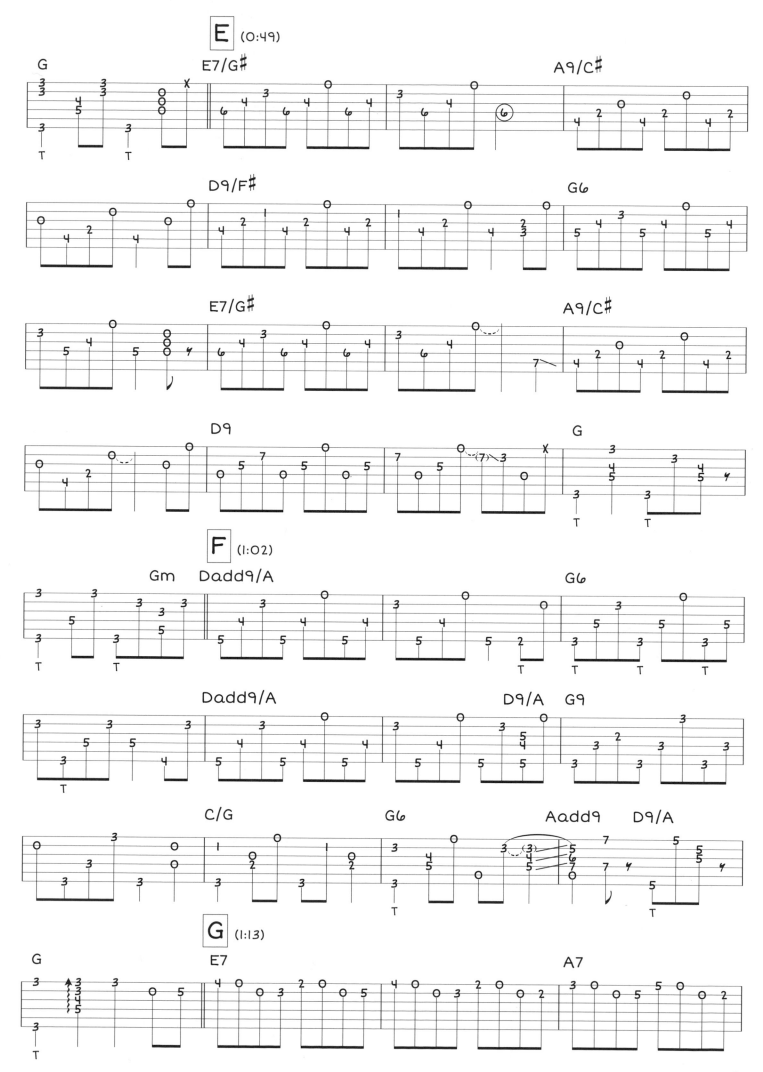

9

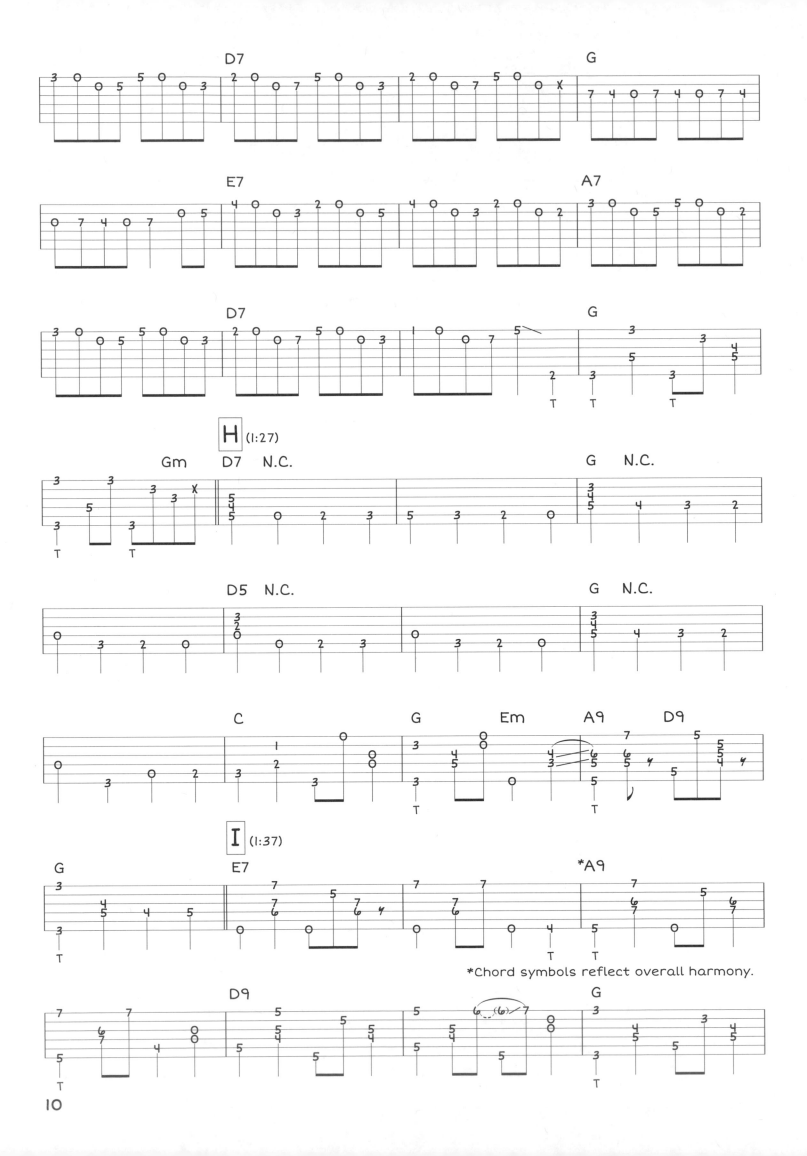

*Chord symbols reflect overall harmony.

10

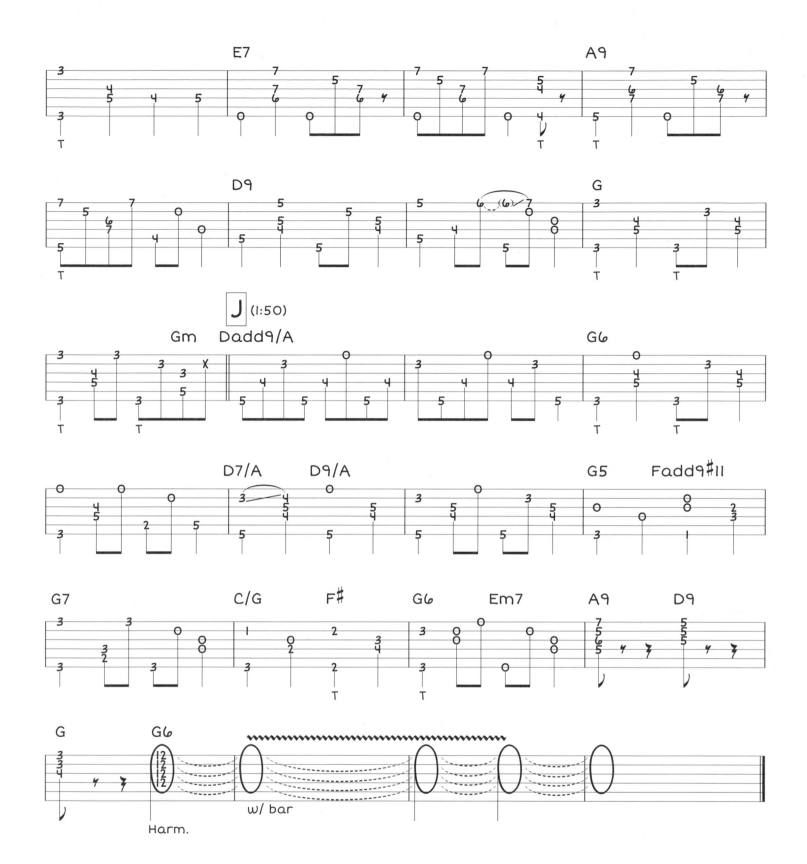

Born in the Dark

Words and Music by Chester Lee Hinesley

Guitar: Dan Huff

Key of G

Intro

Moderately fast

w/ pick & fingers

Verse

You call me

G5	G5	G5	G5	
C5	C5	G5	G5	
D5	D5	G5 N.C.		‖

Interlude

w/ Intro riff

‖: G7	G7	G7	G7	:‖

Verse

Friday I came home

G5	G5	G5	G5	
C5	C5	G5	G5	
D5	D5	G5	G5 A5 A#5 B5	‖

Chorus

Say, hey, sweet baby

|C5 |C5 |G5 |G5 |

|C5 |C5 |A5 |D5   ‖

Guitar Solo

Chorus

Say, hey, sweet baby

|C5 |C5 |G5 |G5 |

|C5 |C5 |A5 |D5 |

|N.C.   ‖

Interlude

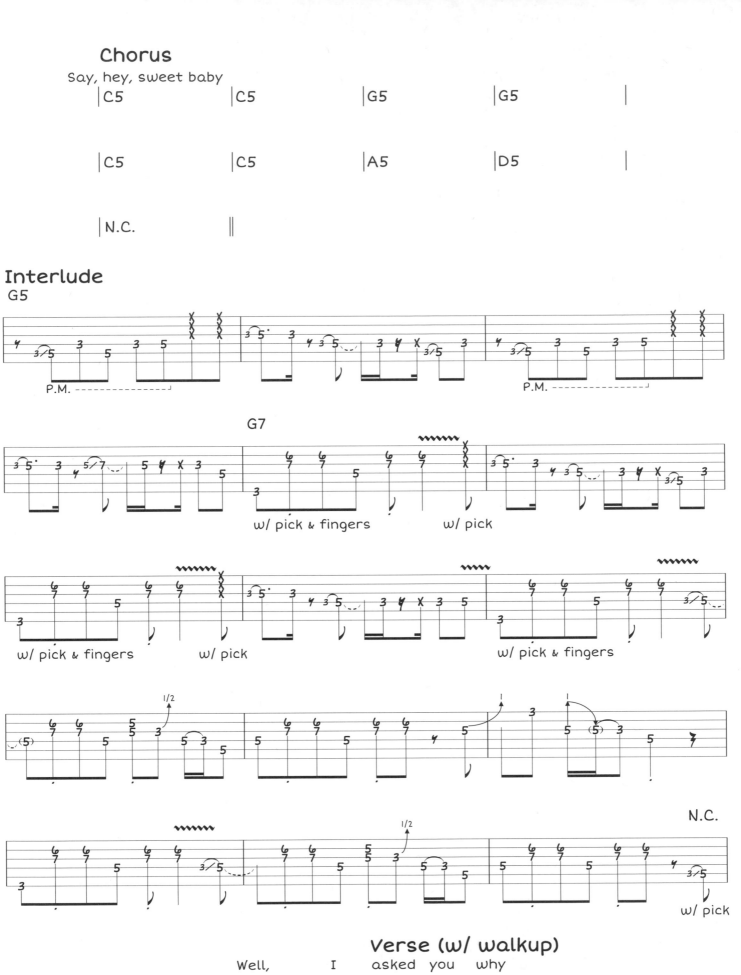

w/ pick & fingers   w/ pick

w/ pick & fingers   w/ pick   w/ pick & fingers

N.C.

w/ pick

Verse (w/ walkup)

Well,   I   asked you   why

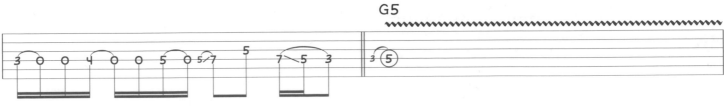

Guitar Solo

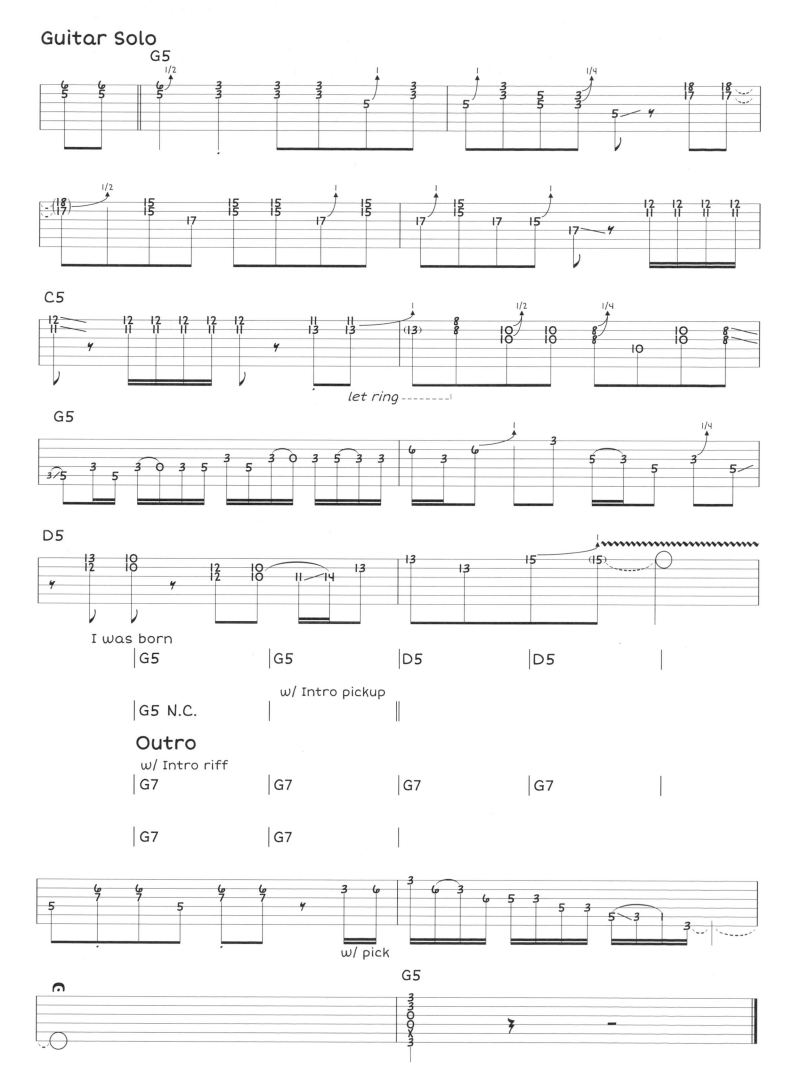

I was born

|G5 |G5 |D5 |D5 |

w/ Intro pickup

|G5 N.C. | ||

Outro

w/ Intro riff

|G7 |G7 |G7 |G7 |

|G7 |G7 |

w/ pick

G5

from Merle Haggard - *Swinging Doors*

The Bottle Let Me Down

Words and Music by Merle Haggard

Guitar: Roy Nichols

Drop D tuning:
(low to high) D-A-D-G-B-E

Key of D

Intro

Moderately (♫ = ♩♪)

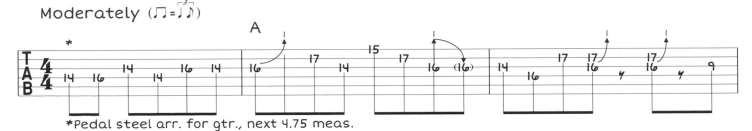

*Pedal steel arr. for gtr., next 4.75 meas.

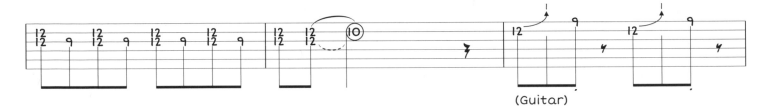

(Guitar)

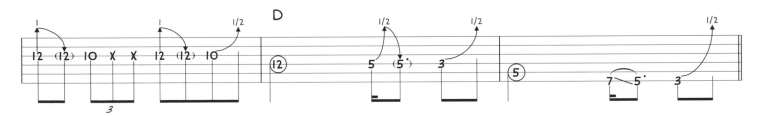

D

Verse

Each night I leave

D	D	D	D	
D	D	A	A	
A	A	A	A	
A	A	D	D	

Chorus

To - night

D	D	D	D	
D	D	A	A	
A	A	A	A	
A	A	D	D	‖

Interlude

w/ Intro riff

| A | A | A | A | |
| A | A | D | D | ‖ |

Ending

D

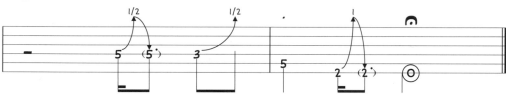

Buckaroo

Words and Music by Ed Hill and Mark D. Sanders

Drop D tuning:
(low to high) D-A-D-G-B-E

Guitar: Brent Mason

Key of D

Intro

Fast

Verse

I ain't lookin'

| D5 | D5 | D5 | D5 | |
| D5 | D5 | D5 | D5 | |

Chorus

I need a man

| G5 | A5 | D5 G5 | G5 | A5 | D5 G5 | |
| G5 | A5 | B5 | G5 | A5 | |

Interlude

w/ Intro riff

| D5 | D5 | D5 | D5 | |

Bridge

Heaven knows

| B♭5 | F5 | C5 | G5 | |
| B♭5 | F5 | A5 | A5 | |

Guitar Solo

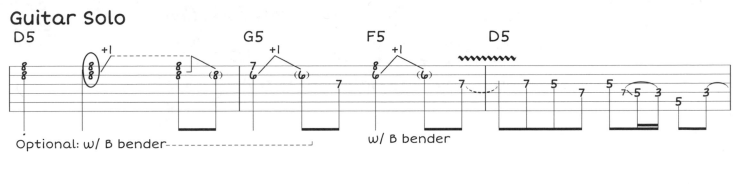

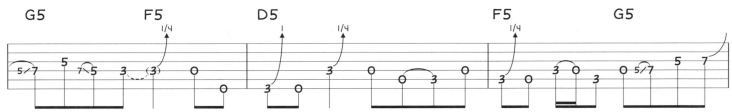

Verse

Don't have to wow me

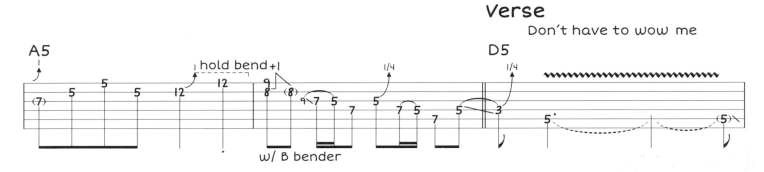

Chorus

If you aspire

‖: G5 |A5   D5 G5 |G5 |A5   D5 G5 |

|G5 |A5   B5 |G5 |G5   :‖

|1.

|2.

|A5   ‖

Outro

w/ Intro riff

Chattahoochee

Words and Music by Jim McBride and Alan Jackson

Guitar: Brent Mason

Key of C

Intro

Fast

N.C.

C

G   1/2   C

G   1/2   C   1/4

Verse

Well, 'way down yonder

| C | | C | | C | | G | C | |

| C | | C | | C | | G | C | ‖

Pre-Chorus

Down by the river

| F | | F | | C | | G | C | |

| F | | F | | D7 | | G | | |

| G | | ‖

Chorus

Yeah, 'way down yonder

| C | | C | | C | | G | C | |

| C | | C | | C | | G | C | ‖

Interlude

w/ Intro riff

| C | | C | | C | | G | C | |

| C | | C | | C | | $\frac{2}{4}$ G | | $\frac{4}{4}$ |

| $\frac{4}{4}$ C | | C | ‖

Guitar Solo

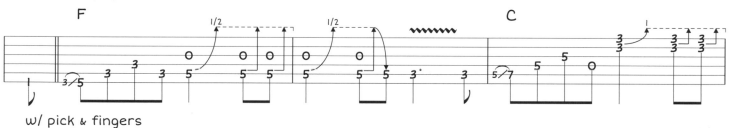

w/ pick & fingers

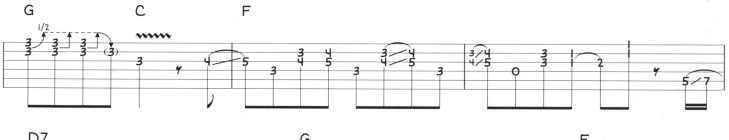

let 2nd string ring -

Fiddle Solo

| F | | F | | C | | G | C | |

| F | | F | | D7 | | G | |

| G | | ‖

Outro

w/ Intro riff

| C | | C | | C | | G | C | |

| C | | C | | C | | $\frac{2}{4}$ G | | $\frac{4}{4}$ |

| $\frac{4}{4}$ C | | ‖

from Jerry Donahue - *Telecasting*

The Claw

By Jerry Reed

Guitar: Jerry Donahue

Key of A

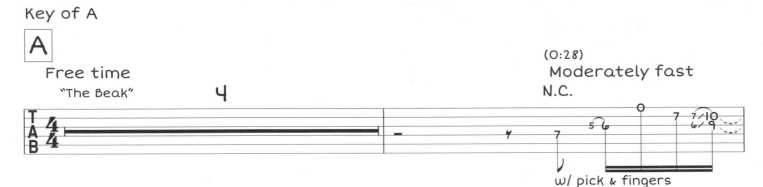

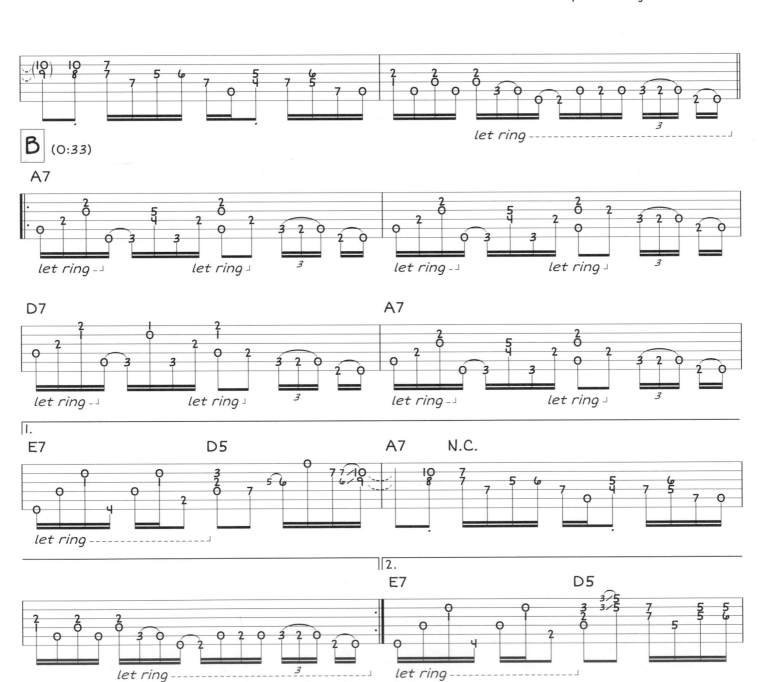

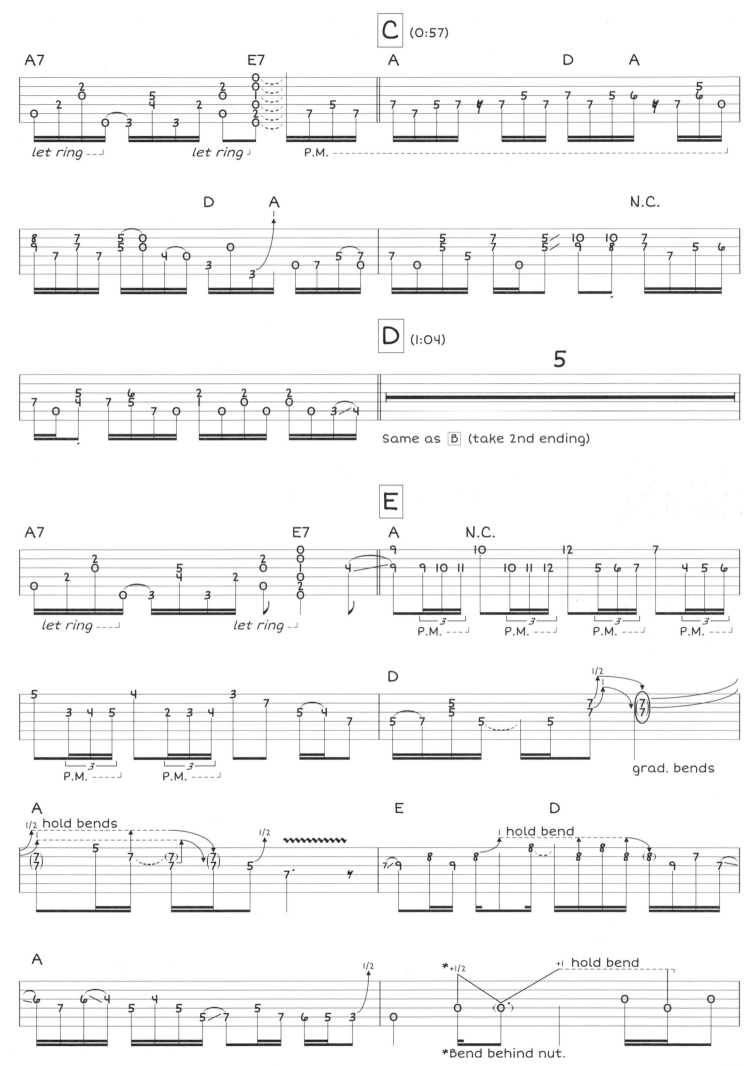

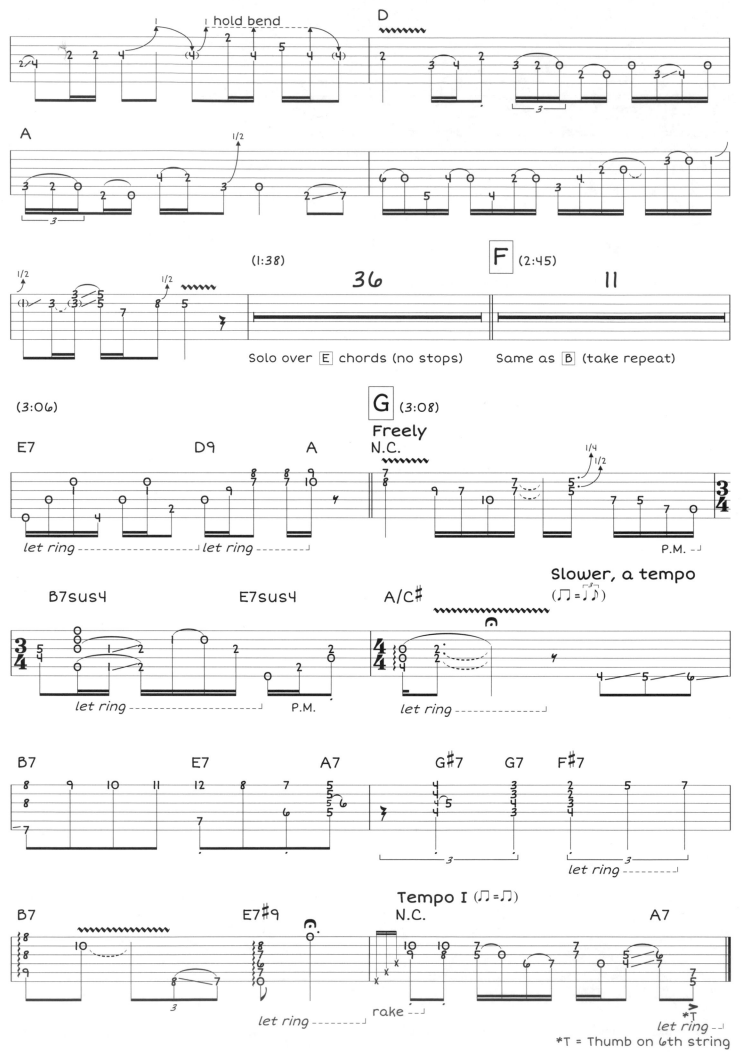

Country Guitar

Words and Music by Phil Baugh and Vern Stovall

Guitar: Phil Baugh

Key of C
Intro
Very fast

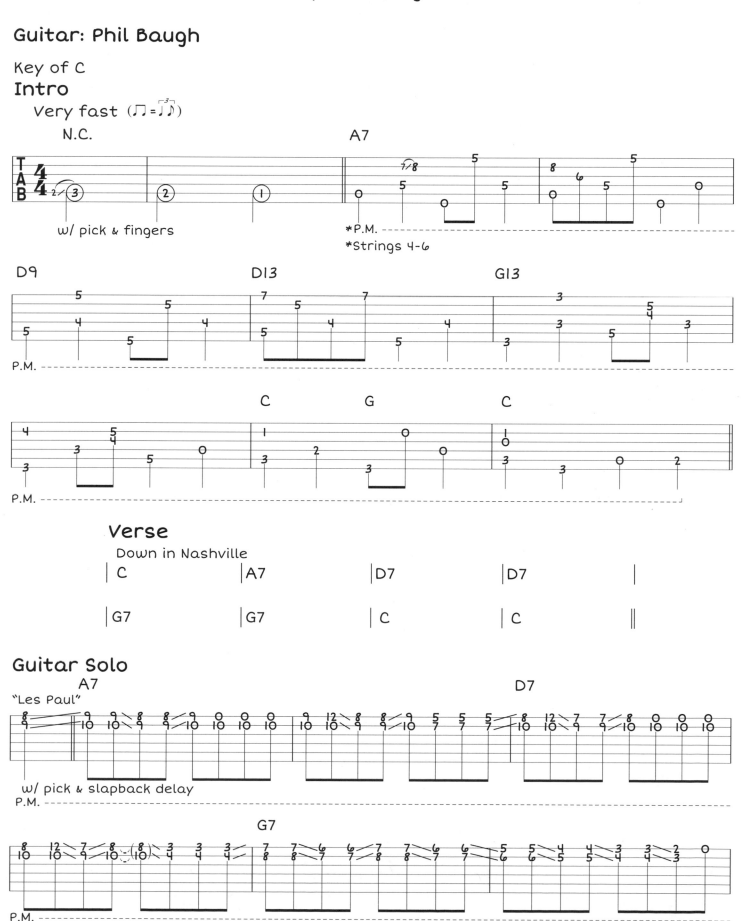

Guitar Solo

"Billy Byrd"

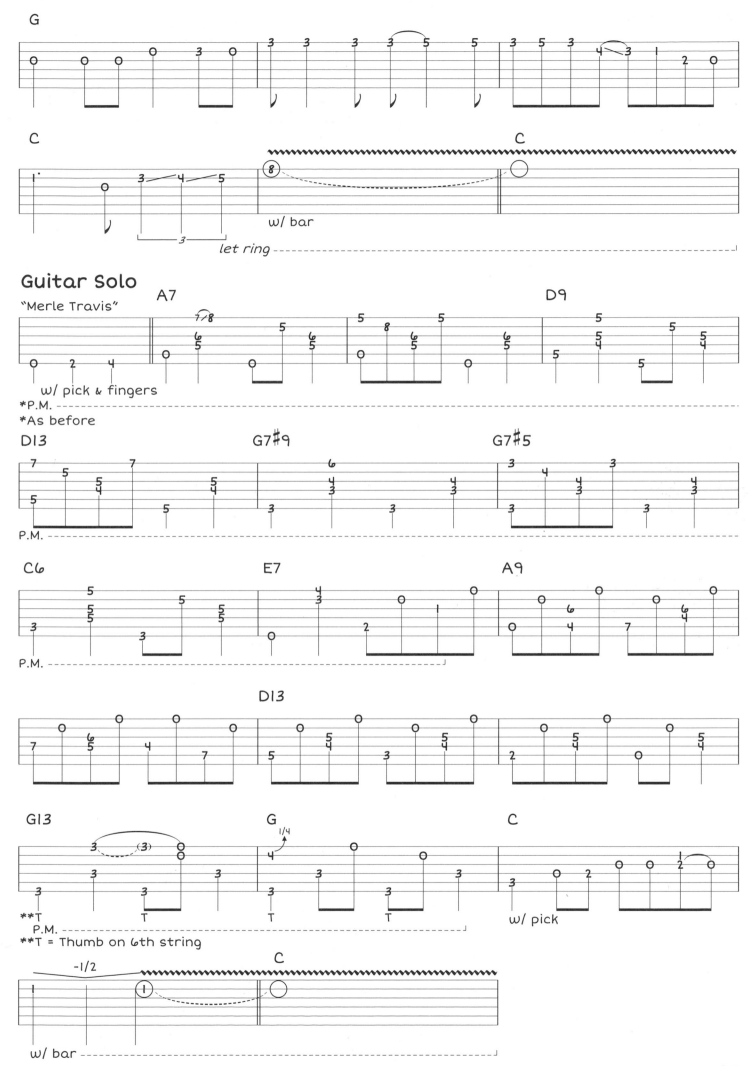

Guitar Solo

"Merle Travis"

w/ pick & fingers
*P.M.
*As before

**T = Thumb on 6th string

Guitar Solo

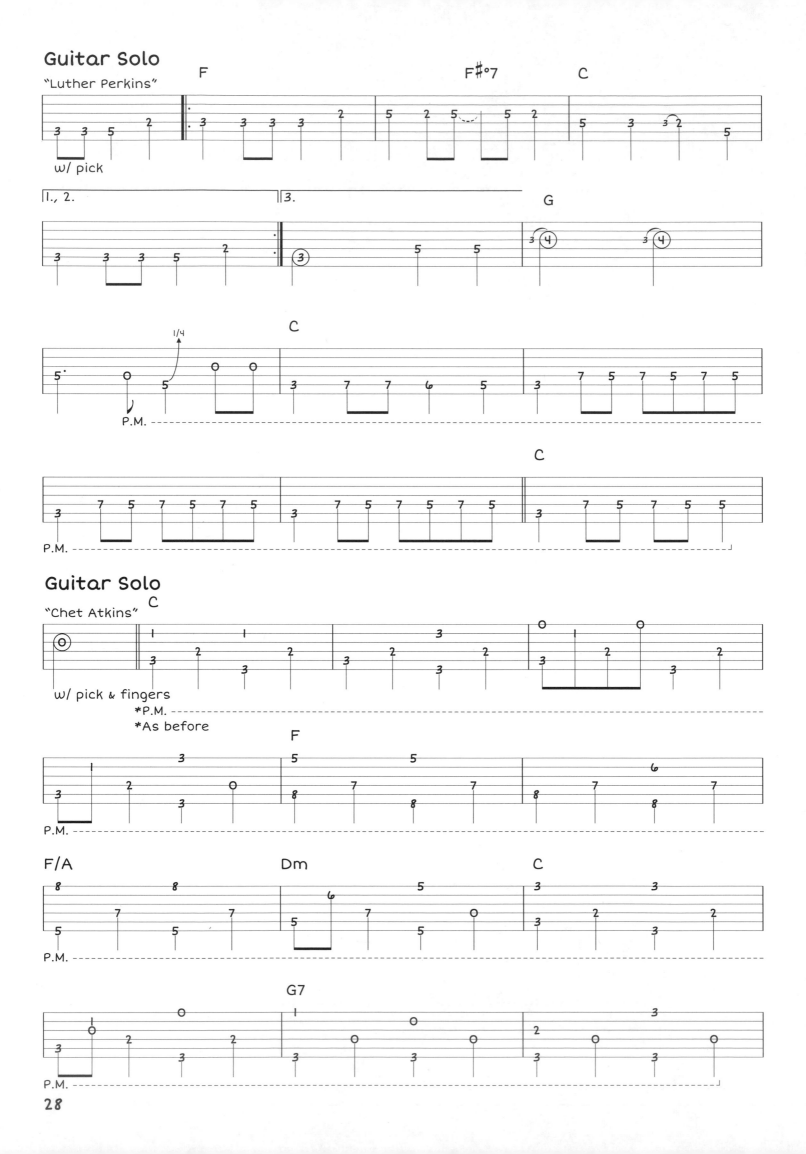

Guitar Solo

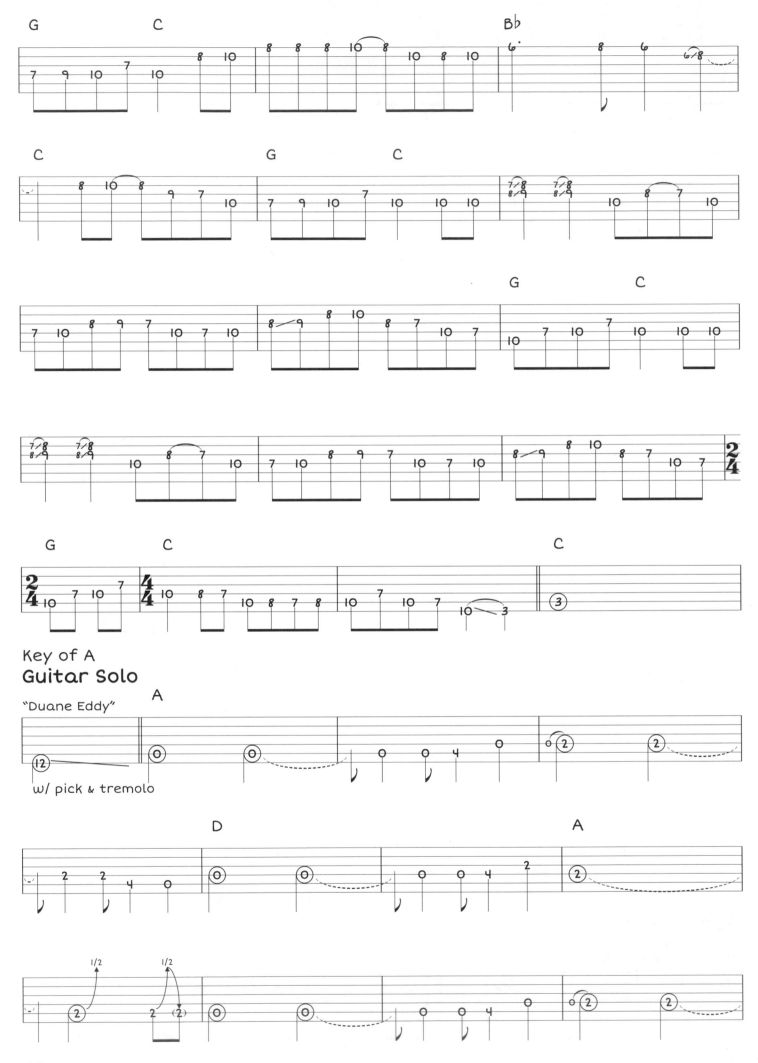

Key of A
Guitar Solo

"Duane Eddy"

w/ pick & tremolo

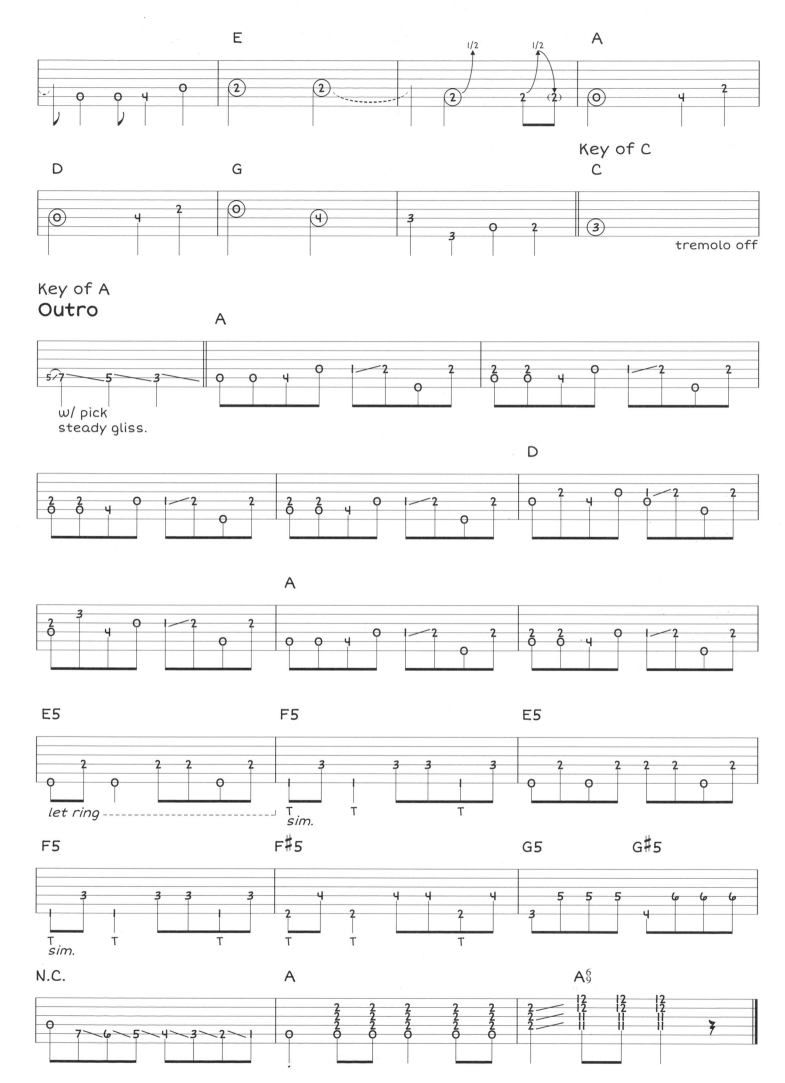

Key of C

Key of A
Outro

tremolo off

w/ pick
steady gliss.

let ring -   sim.

sim.

from Brad Paisley - *Play*

Cluster Pluck

By Brad Paisley, Frank Rogers and Kevin "Swine" Grantt

Guitar: Brad Paisley

Key of A

A (0:00)

Very fast

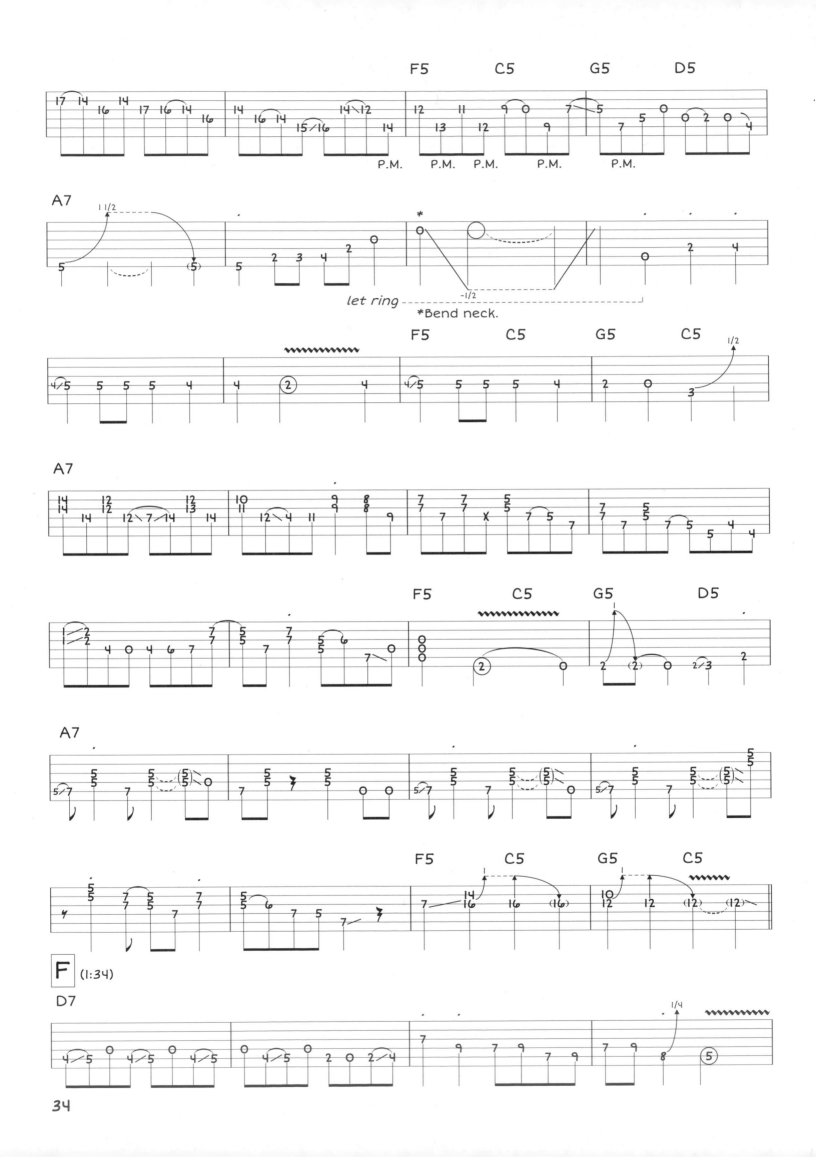

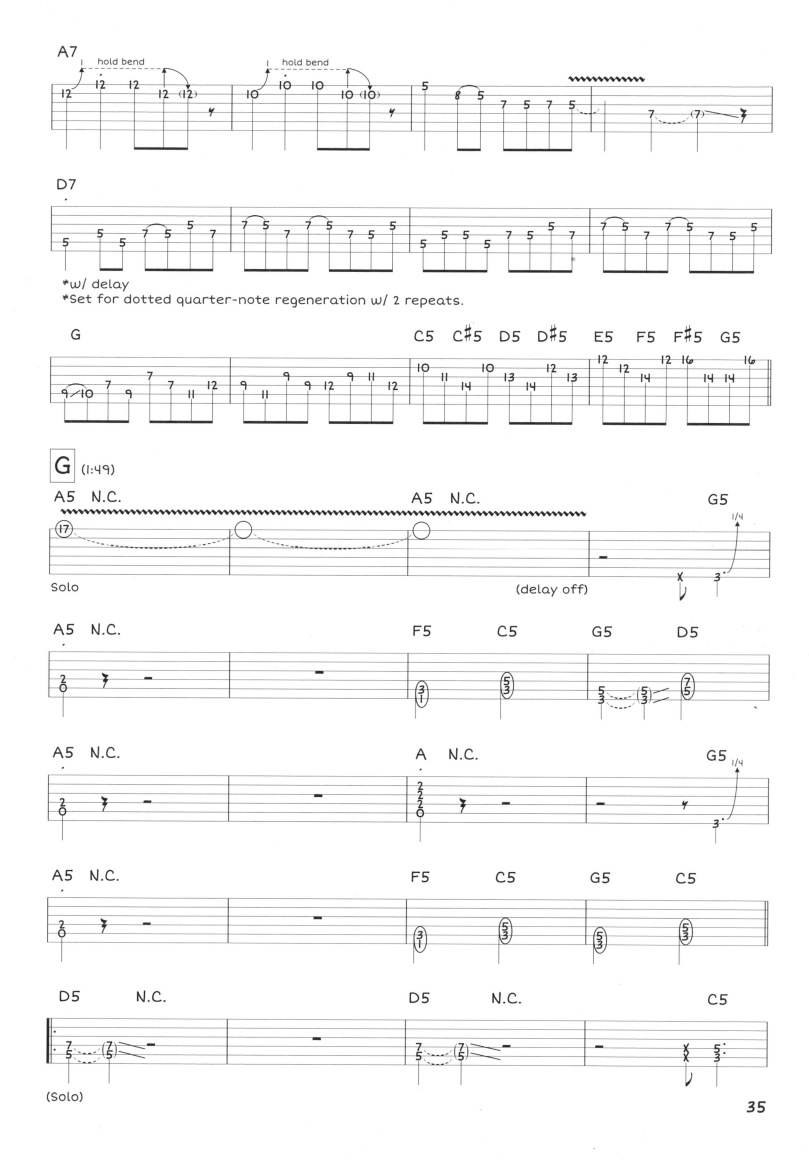

*w/ delay
*Set for dotted quarter-note regeneration w/ 2 repeats.

Solo

(delay off)

(Solo)

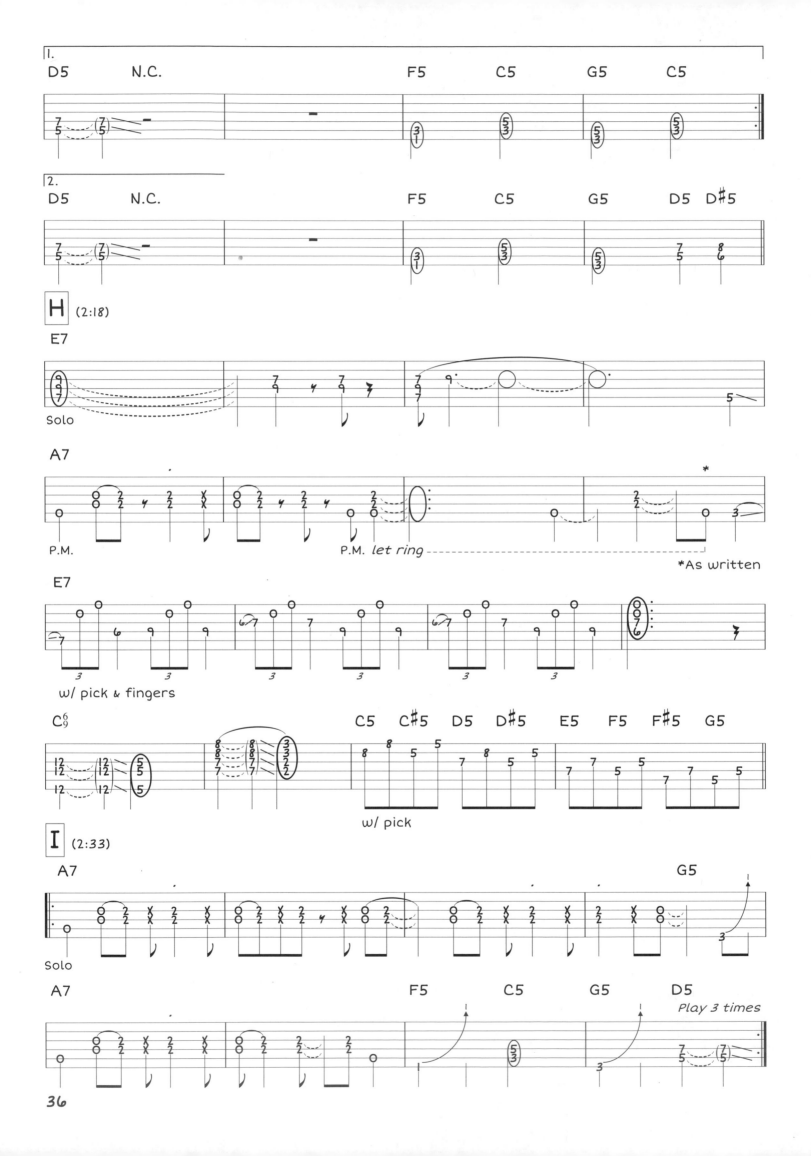

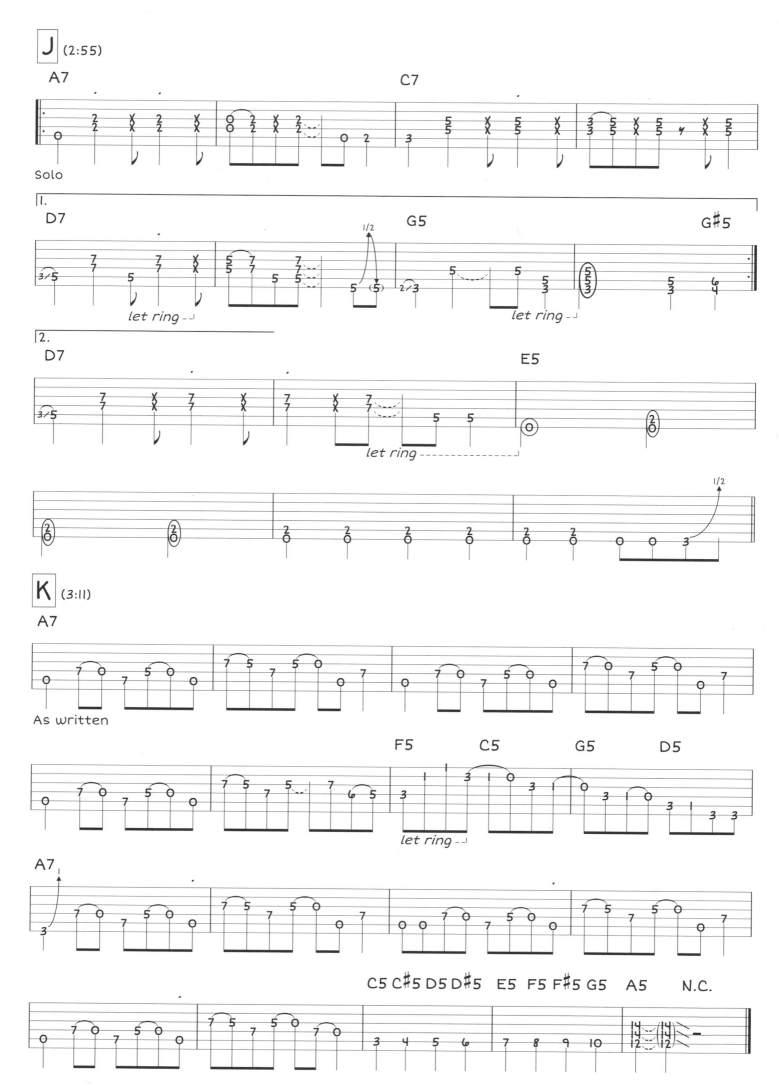

from Keith Urban - *The Ranch*

Clutterbilly

Words and Music by Keith Urban, Peter Clarke and Gregory Holden

Guitar: Keith Urban

Key of A

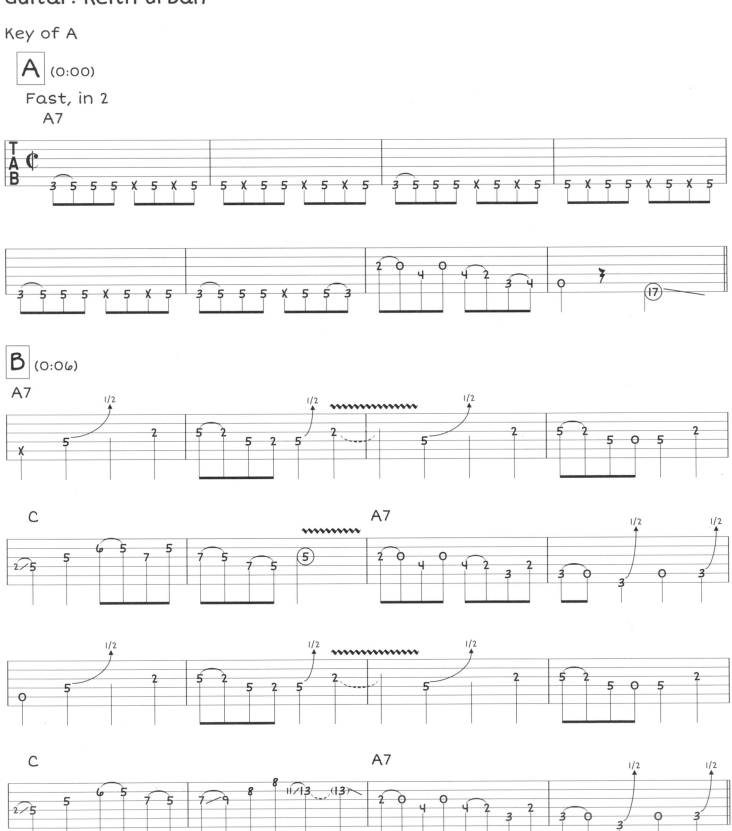

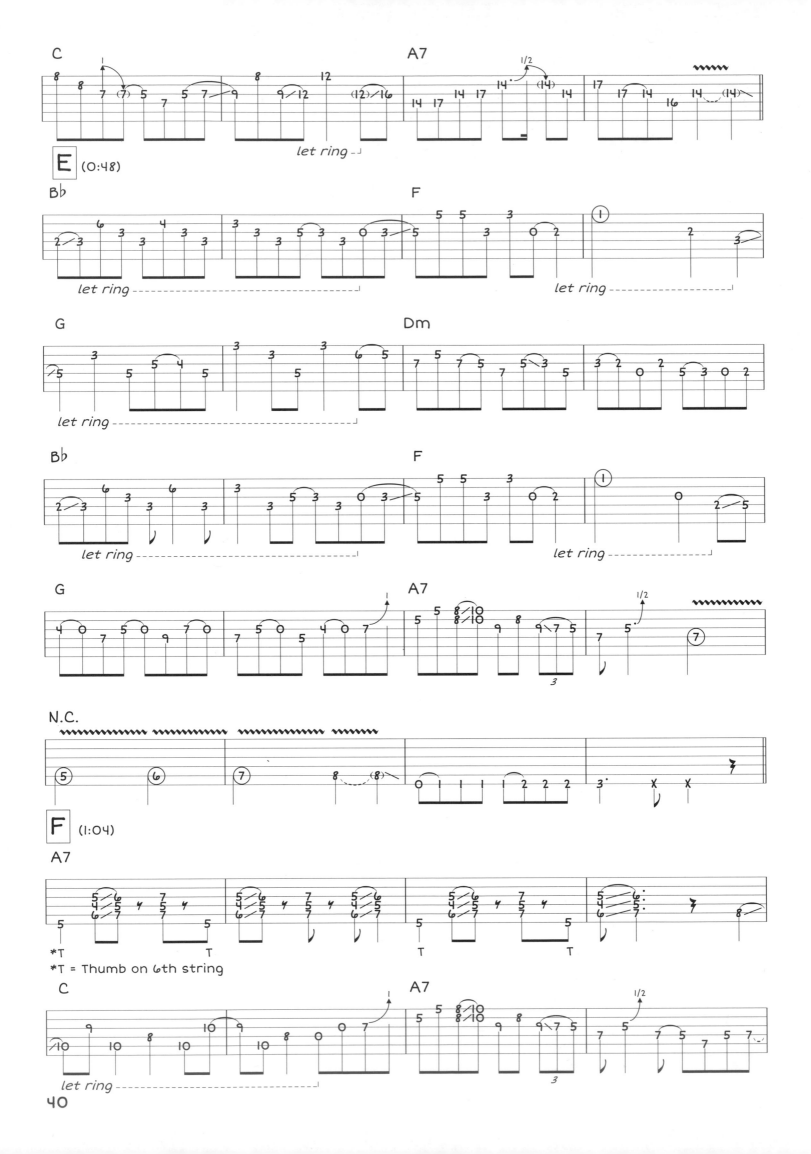

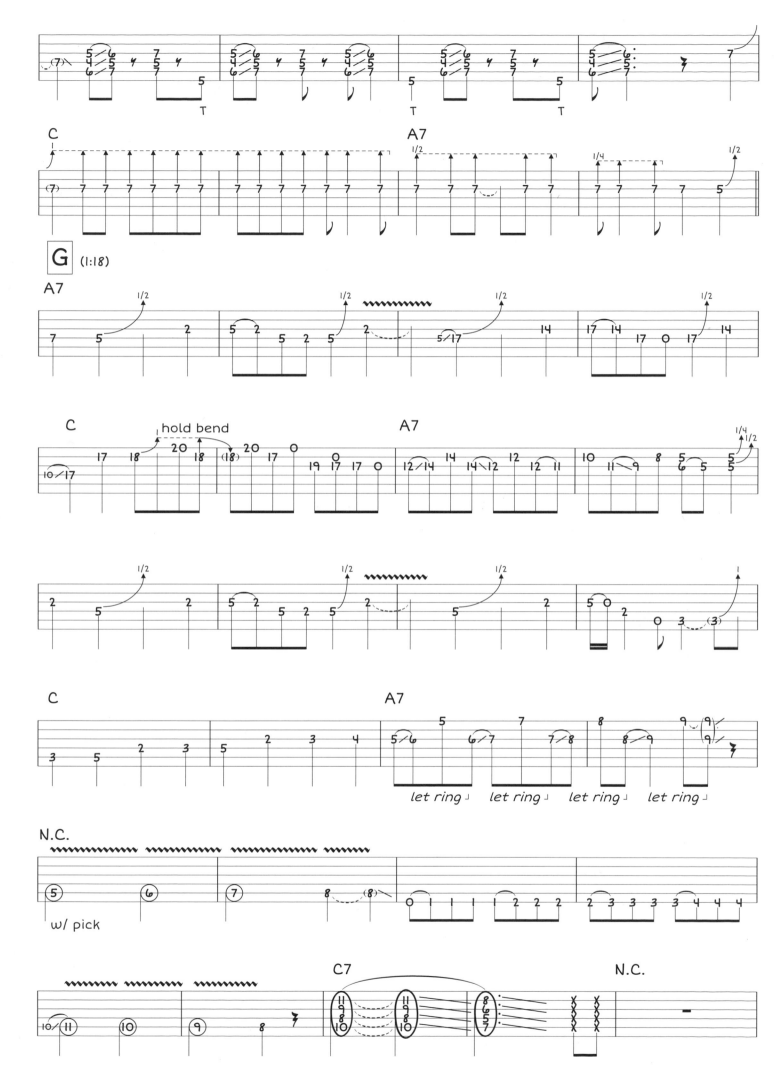

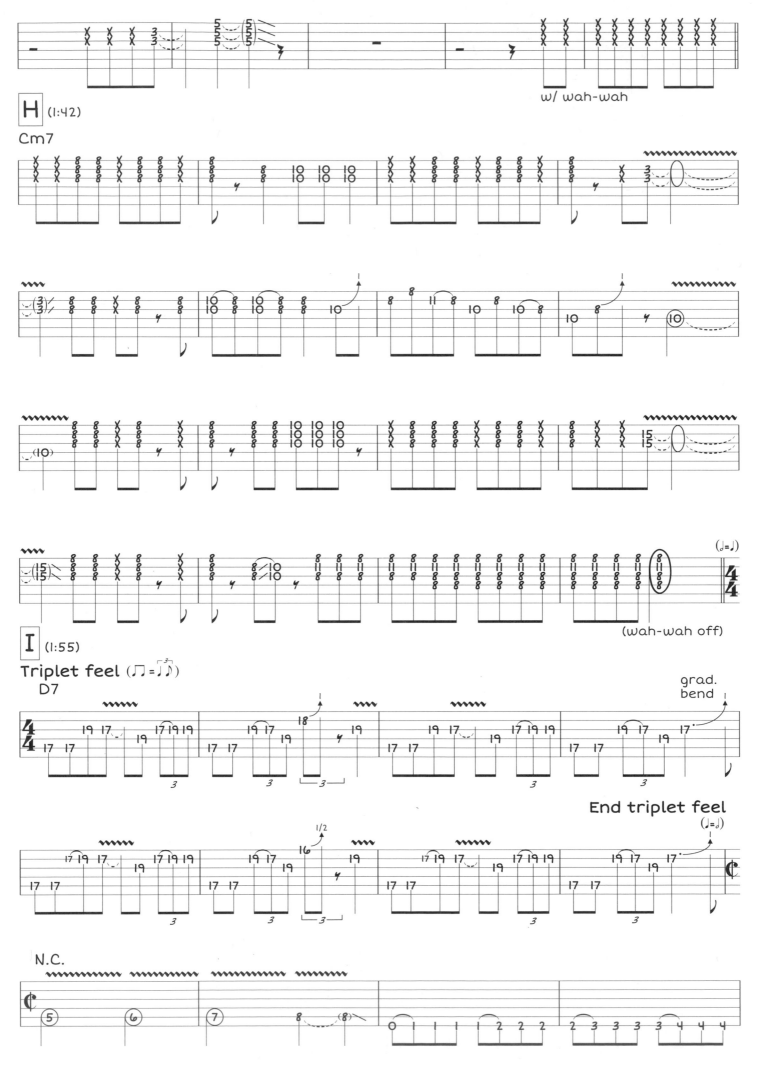

w/ wah-wah

H (1:42)

Cm7

(wah-wah off)

I (1:55)

Triplet feel (♫ = ♪♪³)

D7

grad. bend

End triplet feel

N.C.

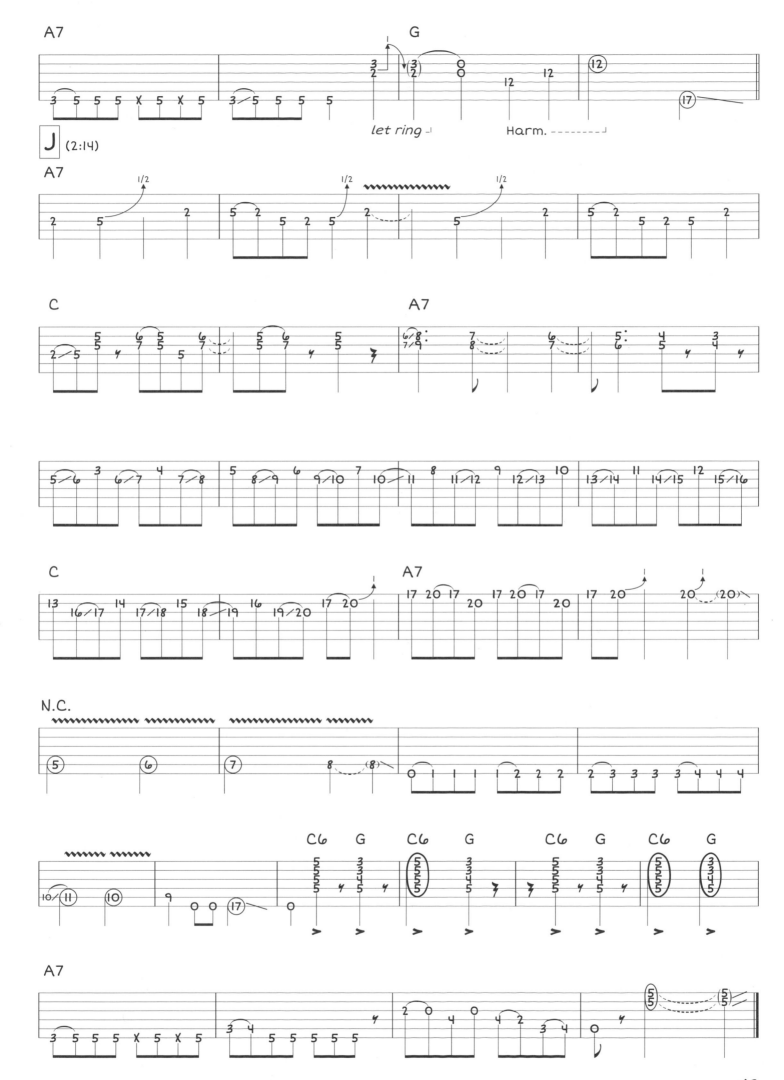

from Mary Chapin Carpenter - *Shooting Straight in the Dark*

Down at the Twist and Shout
Words and Music by Mary Chapin Carpenter

Guitar: John Jennings

Key of A

Intro

Very fast

N.C.

Chorus

Saturday night

D		D		A		A	
E		E		A		A	
D		D	E	A		A	
E		E		A		A	

Verse

And I never have wandered

E		E		A		A	
E		E		A		A	
F#7		F#7		B7		B7	
E		E		E		A	

Solos

D		D		A		A	
E		E		A		A	

Guitar Solo

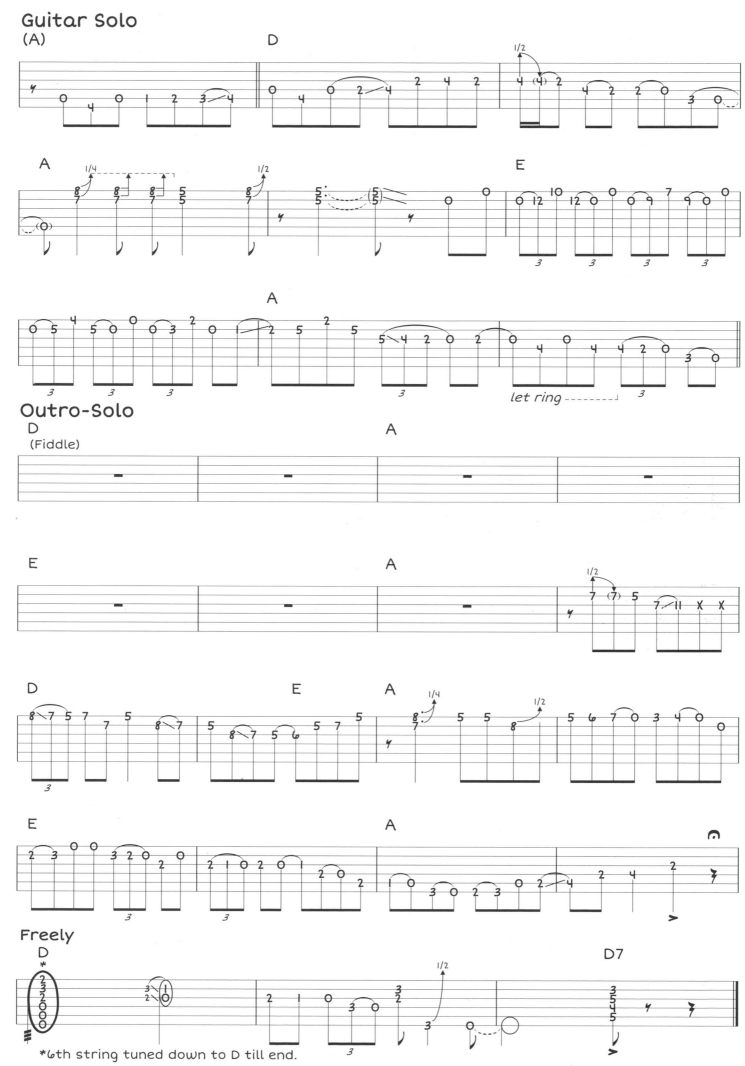

Outro-Solo

*6th string tuned down to D till end.

Flying Fingers

By Joe Maphis

Guitar: Joe Maphis

Key of E

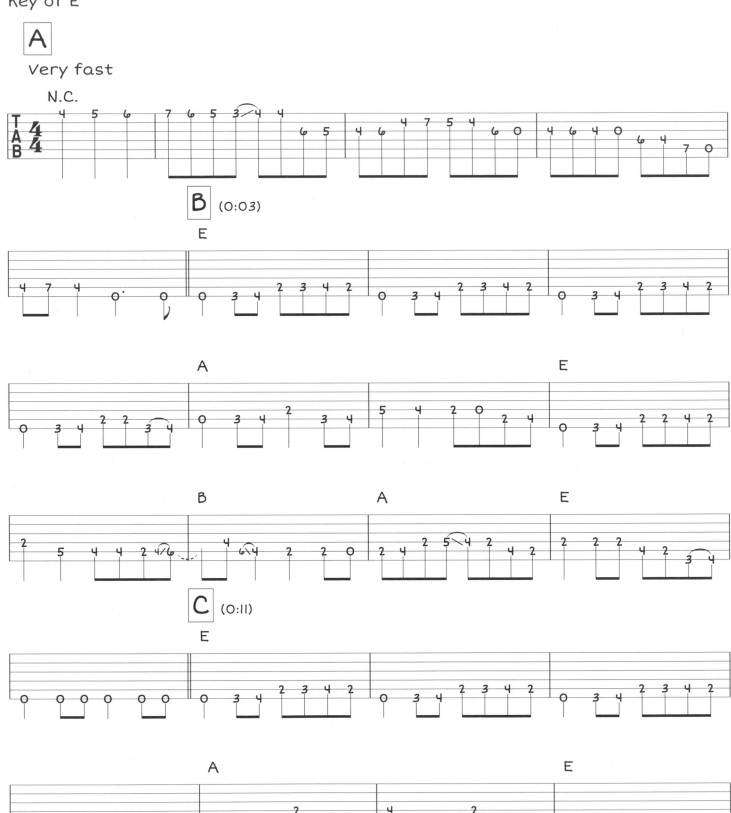

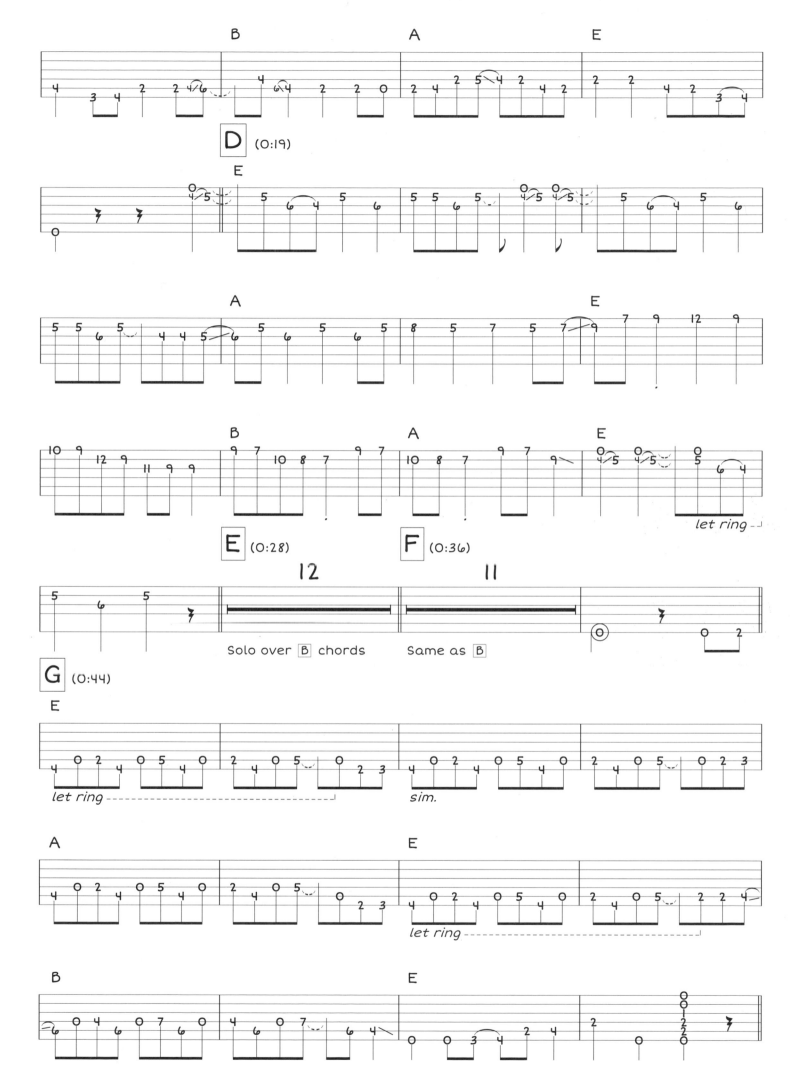

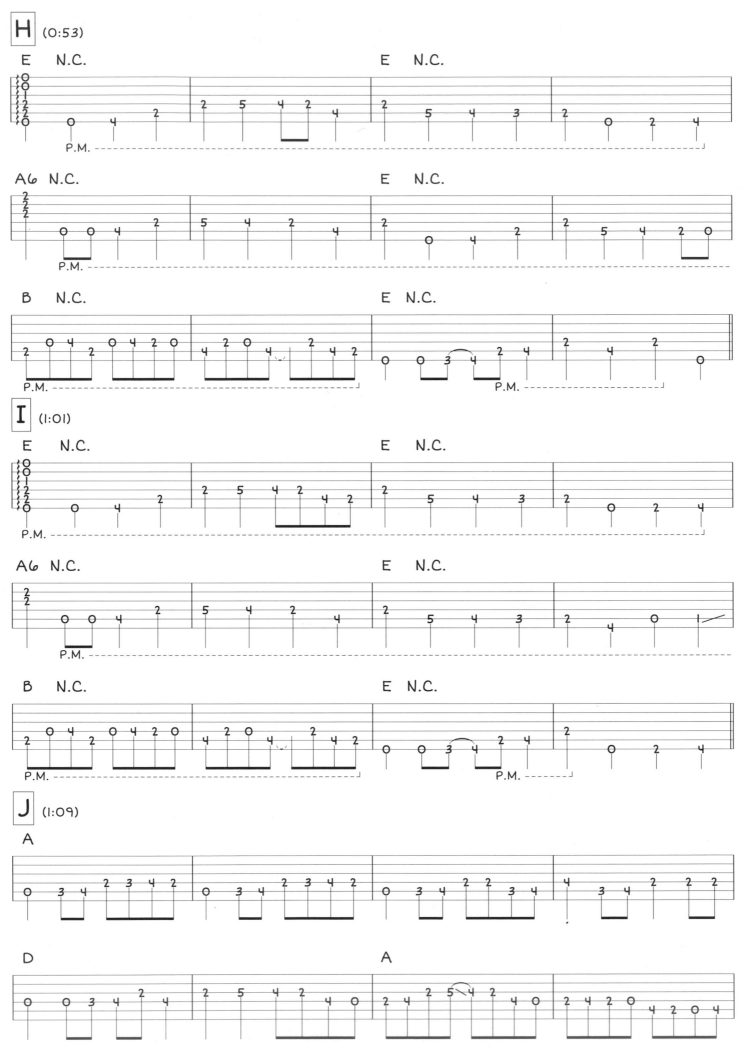

48

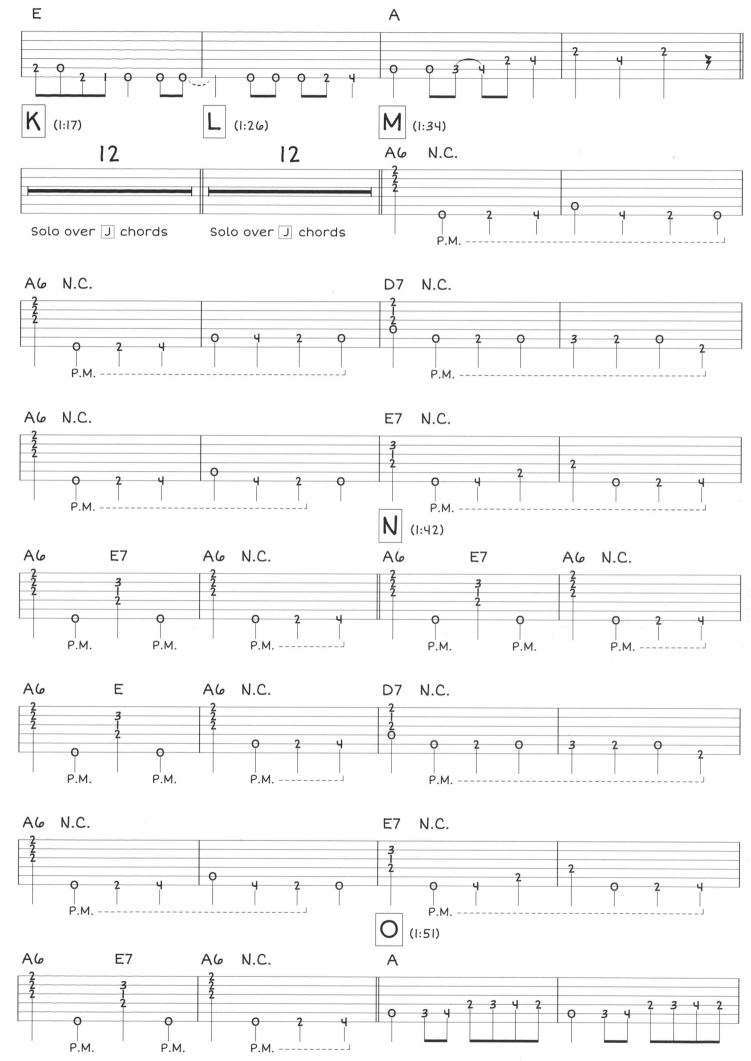

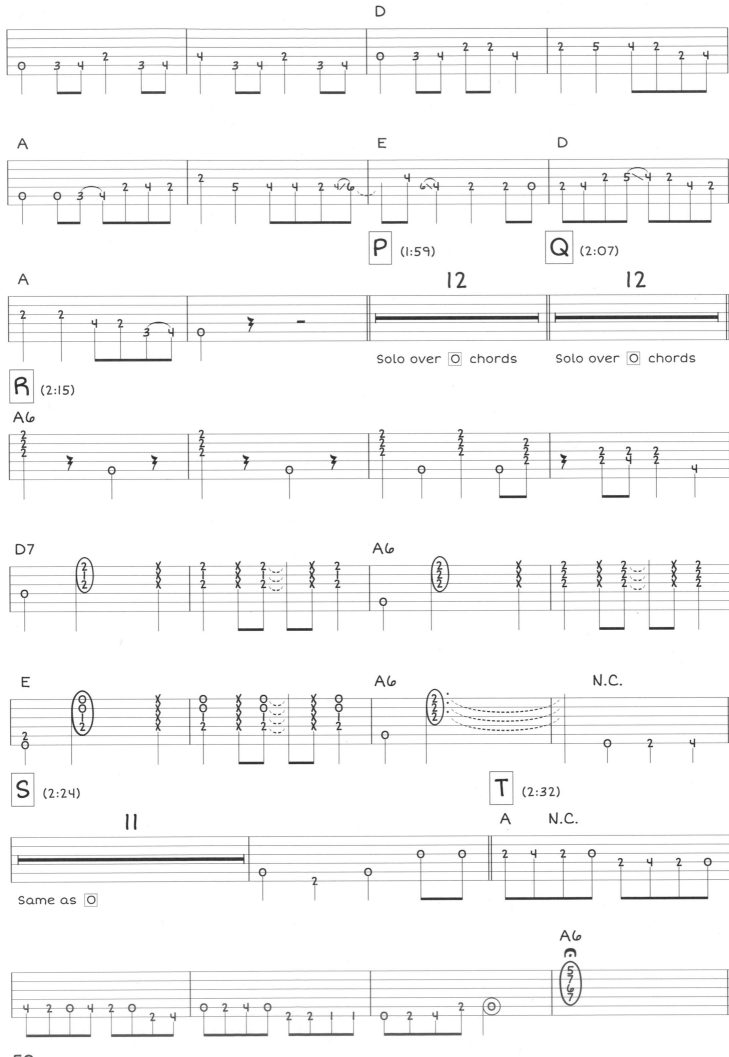

Hot Wired

By Brent Mason and Paul Hollowell

Guitar: Brent Mason

Tune up 1/2 step:
(low to high) E#-A#-D#-G#-B#-E#

Key of A

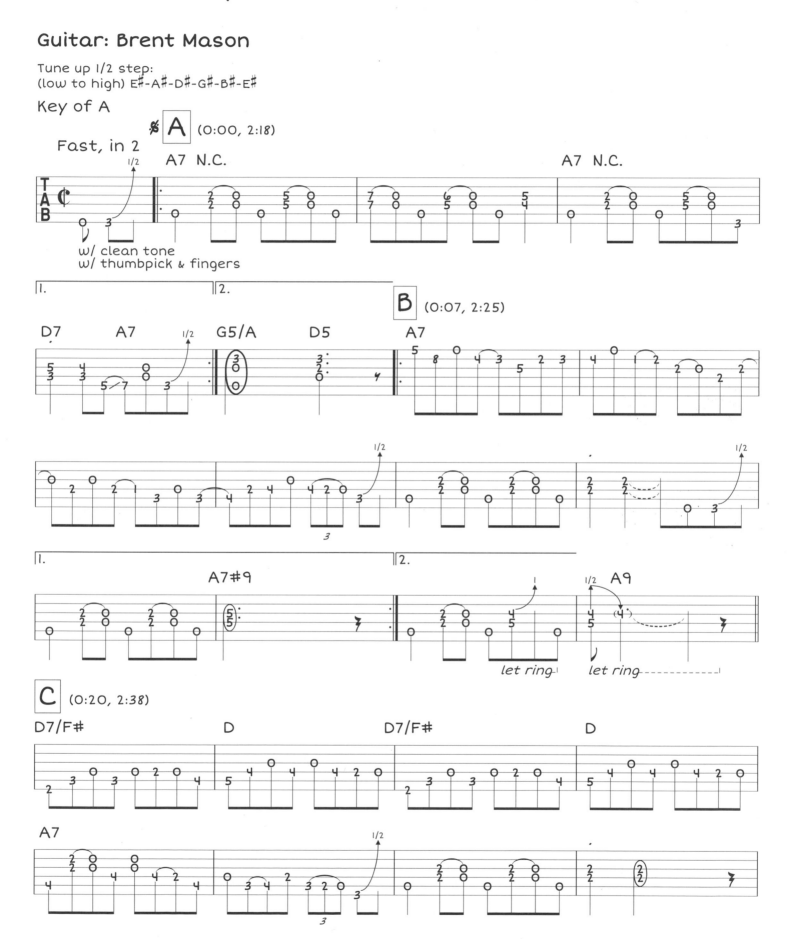

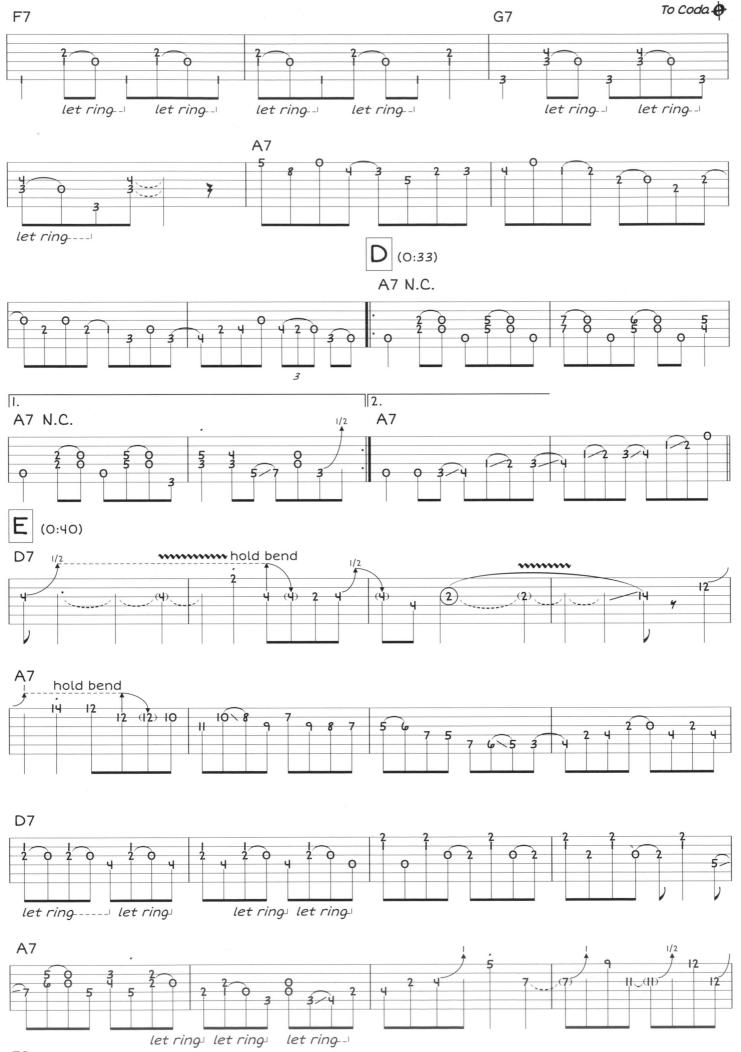

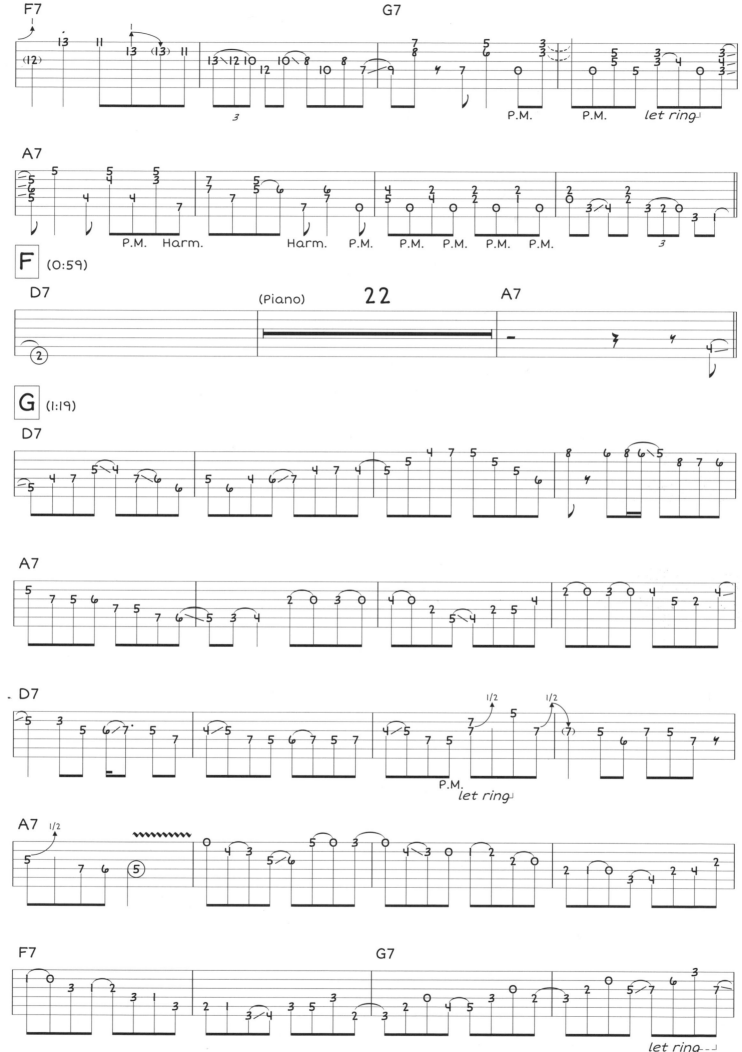

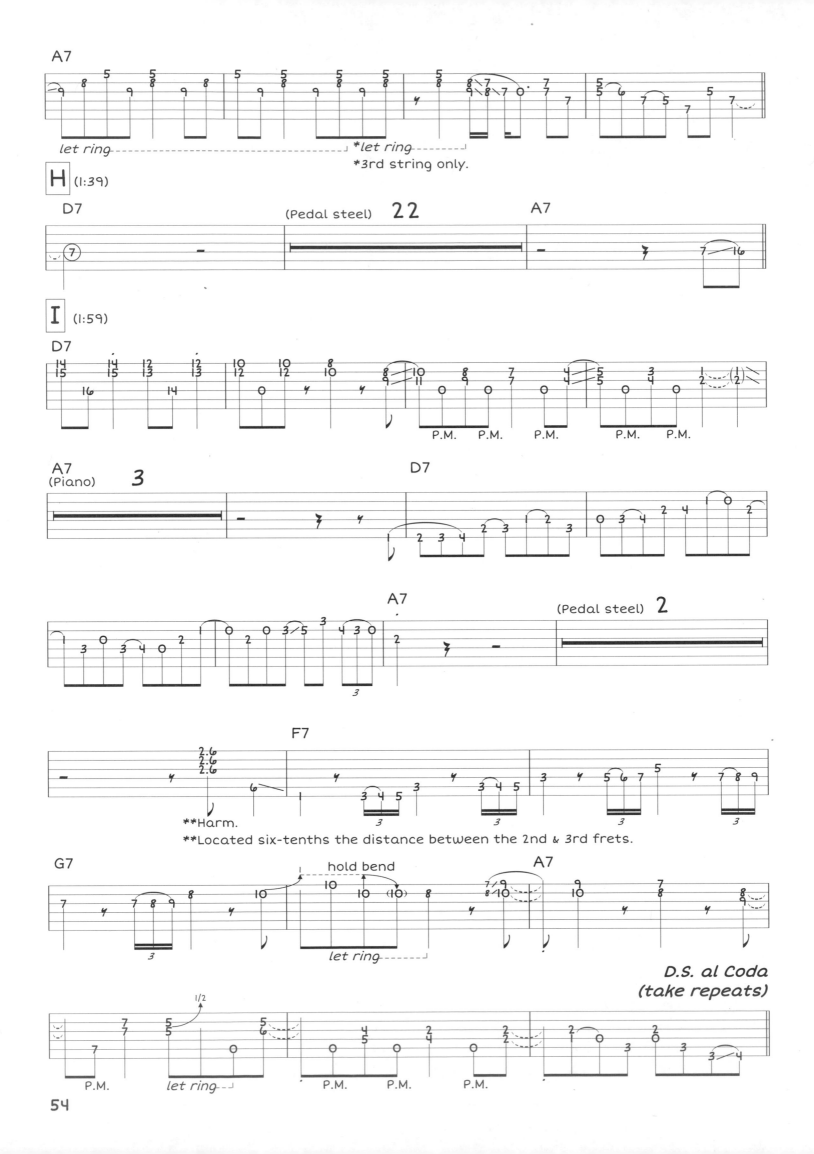

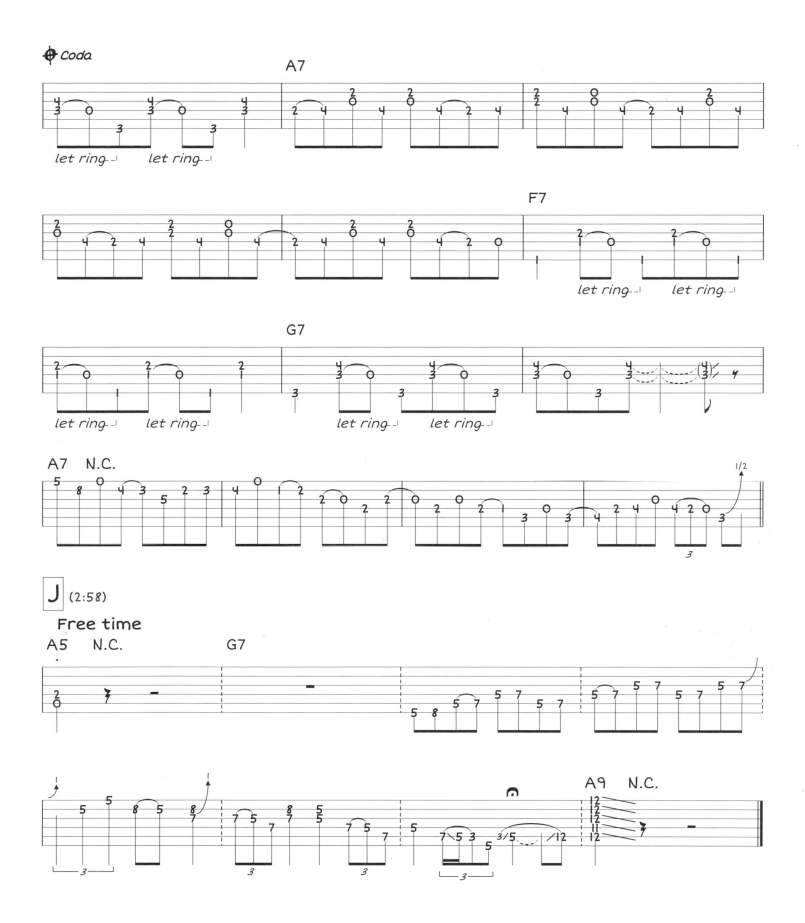

Foggy Mountain Breakdown

By Earl Scruggs

**Guitar: Randy Scruggs,
Vince Gill, Albert Lee**

Key of G

Head (0:00)

Fast, in 2

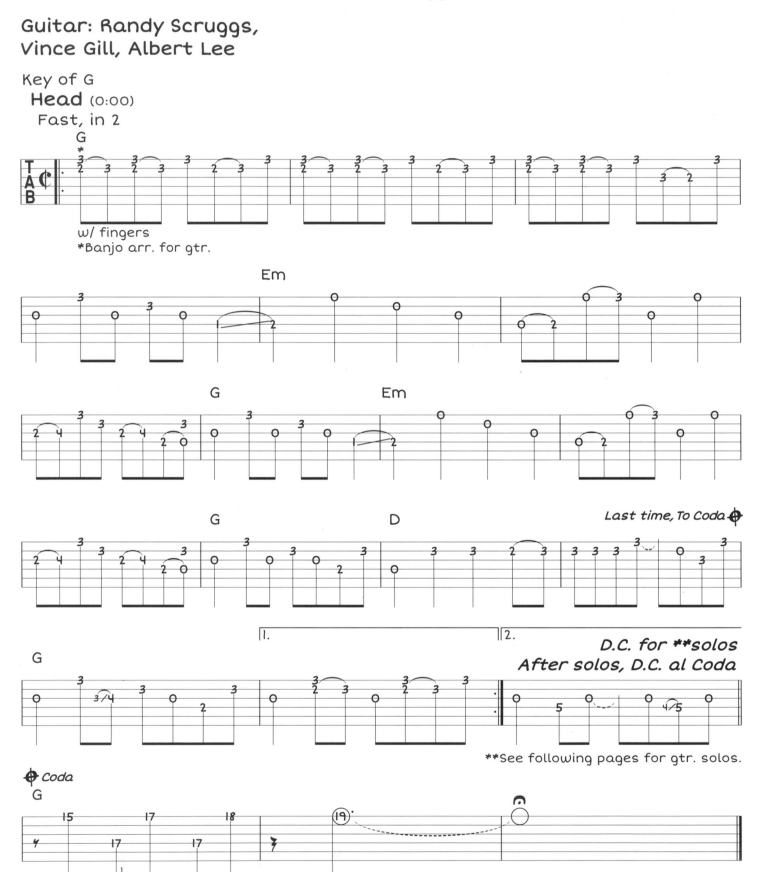

w/ fingers
*Banjo arr. for gtr.

**See following pages for gtr. solos.

Guitar Solo I (0:48)

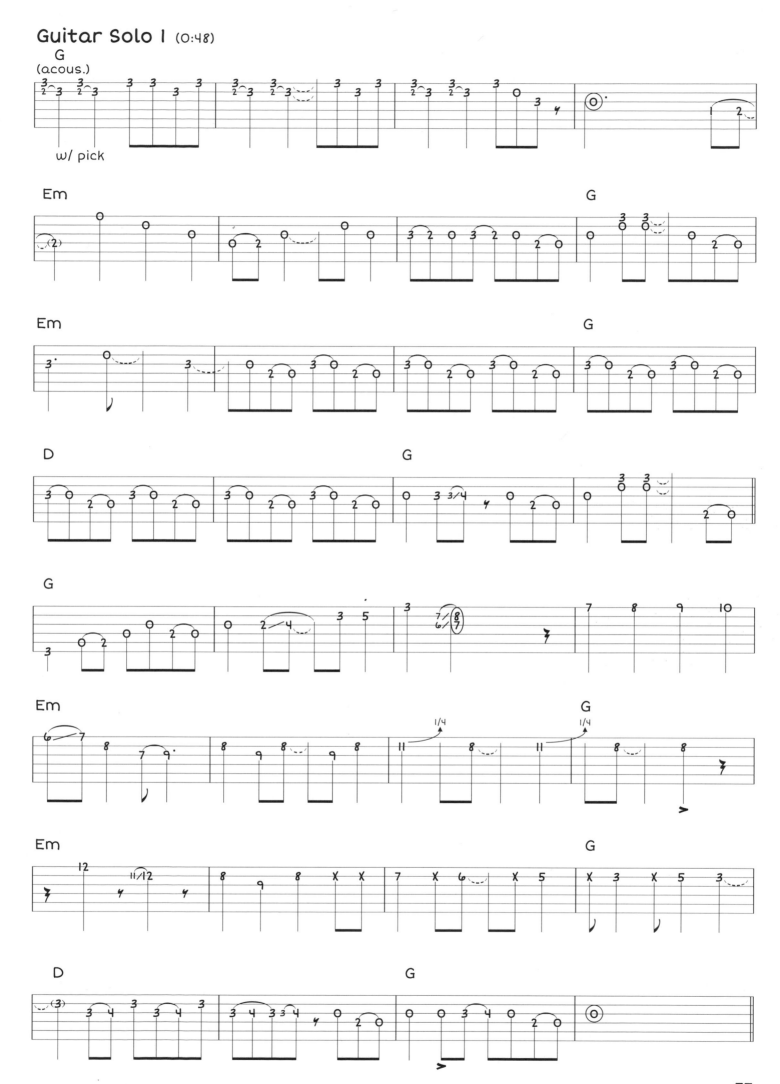

Guitar Solo 2 (1:36)

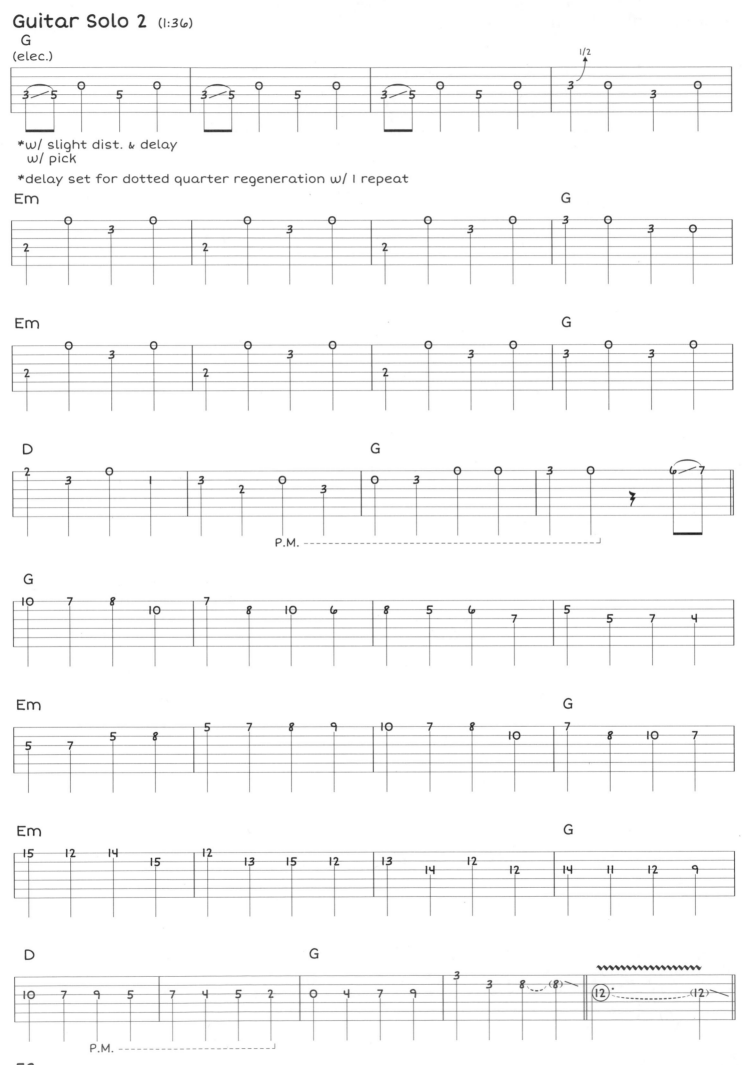

*w/ slight dist. & delay
w/ pick

*delay set for dotted quarter regeneration w/ 1 repeat

58

Guitar Solo 3 (2:24)

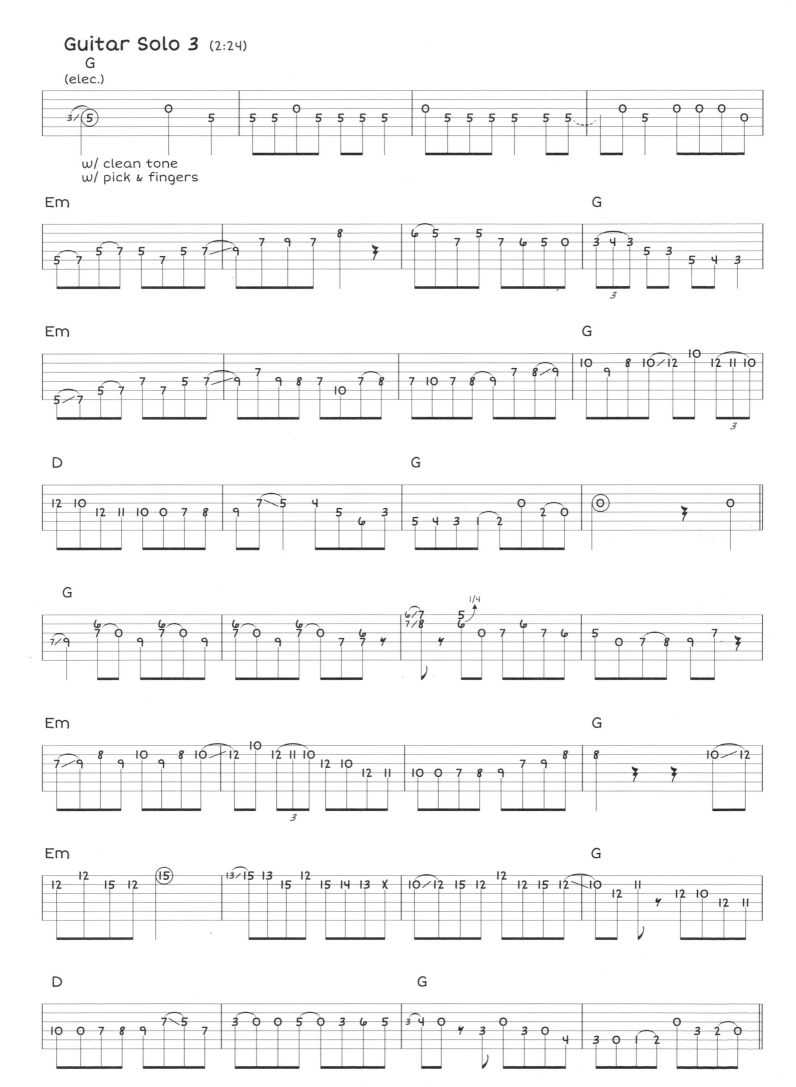

Folsom Prison Blues

Words and Music by John R. Cash

Guitar: Luther Perkins

Key of E (Capo I)
Intro/Outro
Moderately, in 2

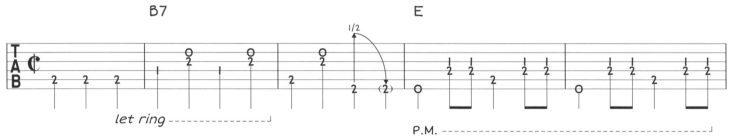

Verse

I hear the train a comin'

E	E	E	E	
E	E	E	E	
A	A	A	A	
E	E	E	E	
B7	B7	B7	B7	
E	E	‖		

Guitar Solo

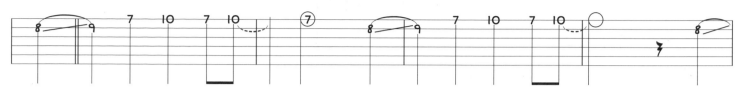

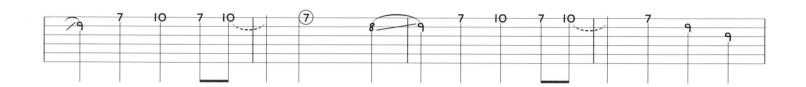

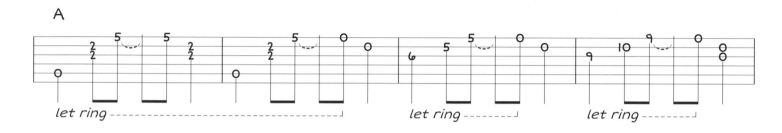

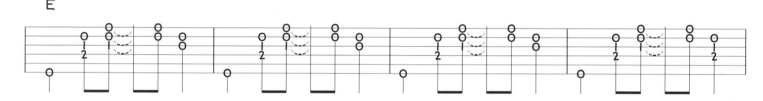

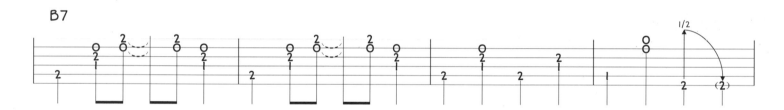

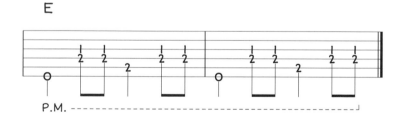

from Albert Lee - *Gagged but Not Bound*

Fun Ranch Boogie

Words and Music by Albert Lee and Sterling Ball

Guitar: Albert Lee

Key of E

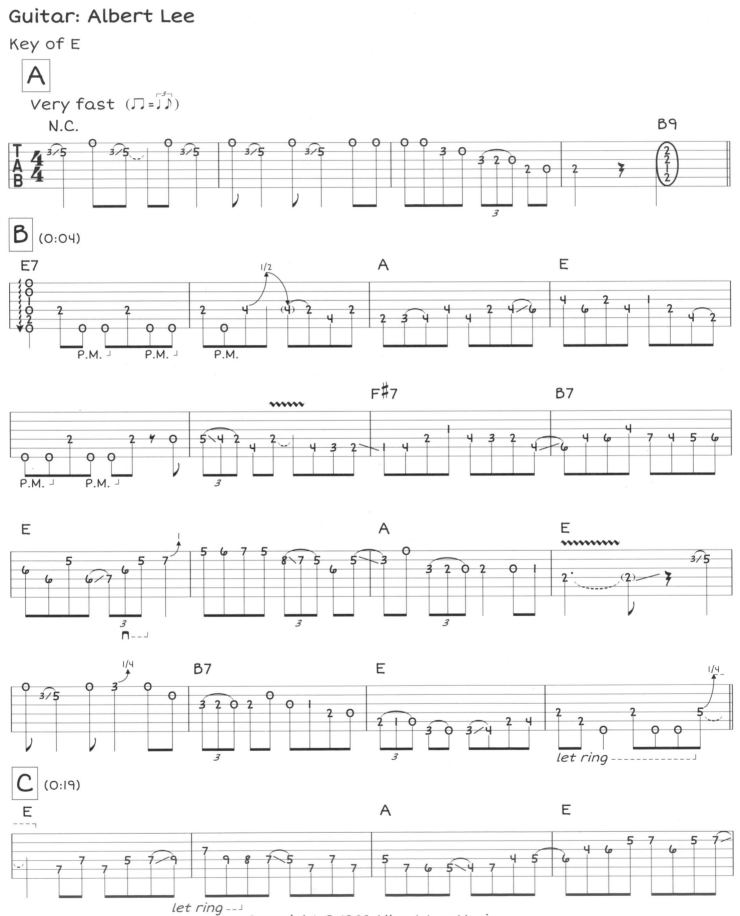

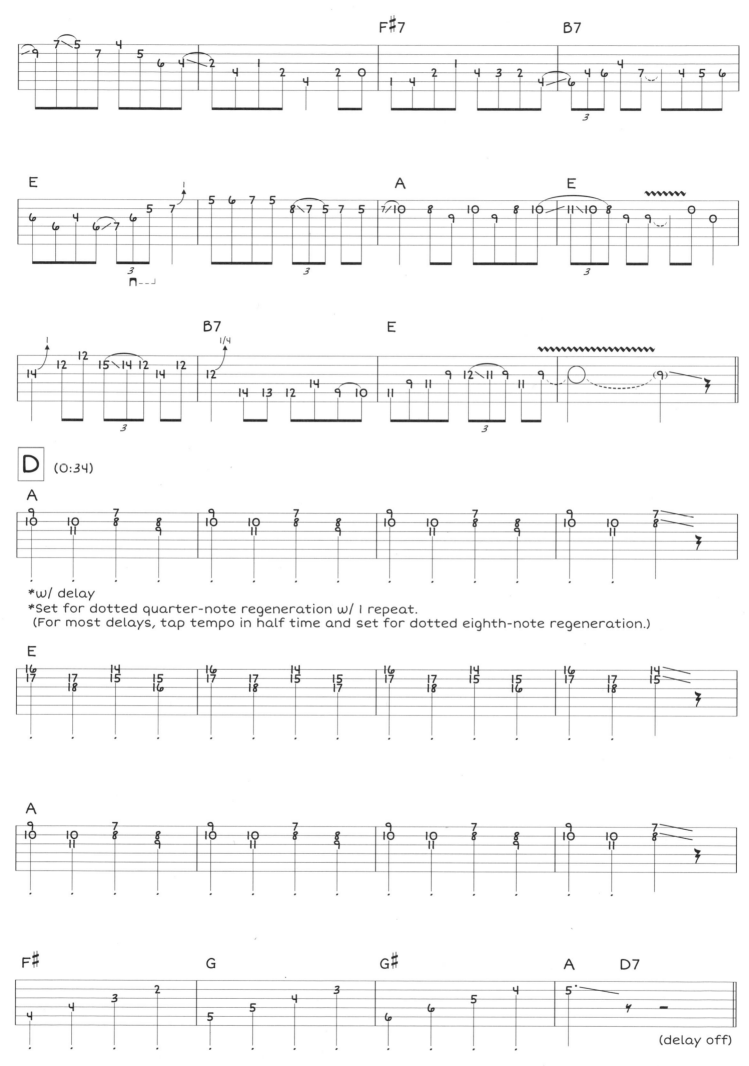

*w/ delay
*Set for dotted quarter-note regeneration w/ 1 repeat.
 (For most delays, tap tempo in half time and set for dotted eighth-note regeneration.)

(delay off)

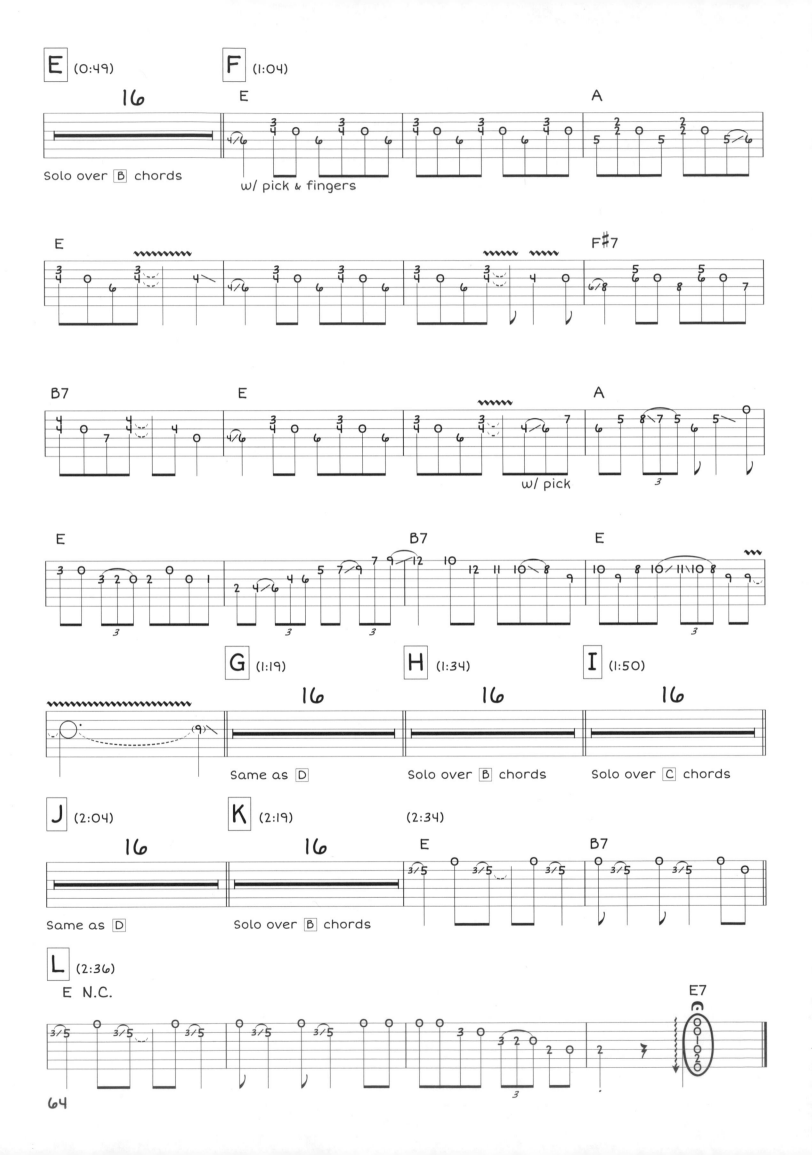

from Danny Gatton - *88 Elmira St.*

Funky Mama

By John Patton

Guitar: Danny Gatton

Key of G

Intro

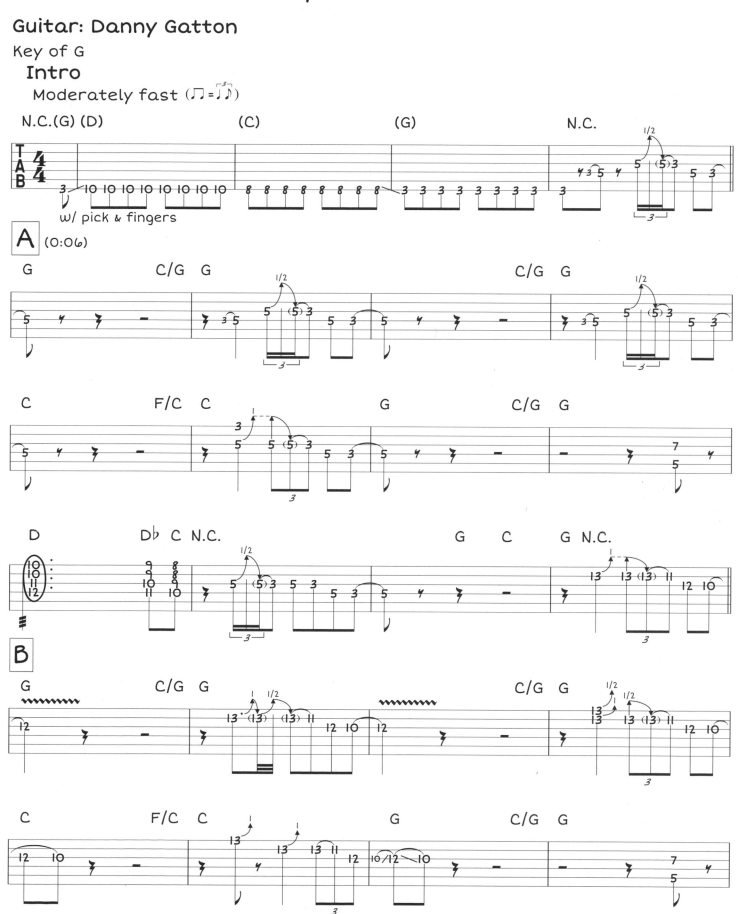

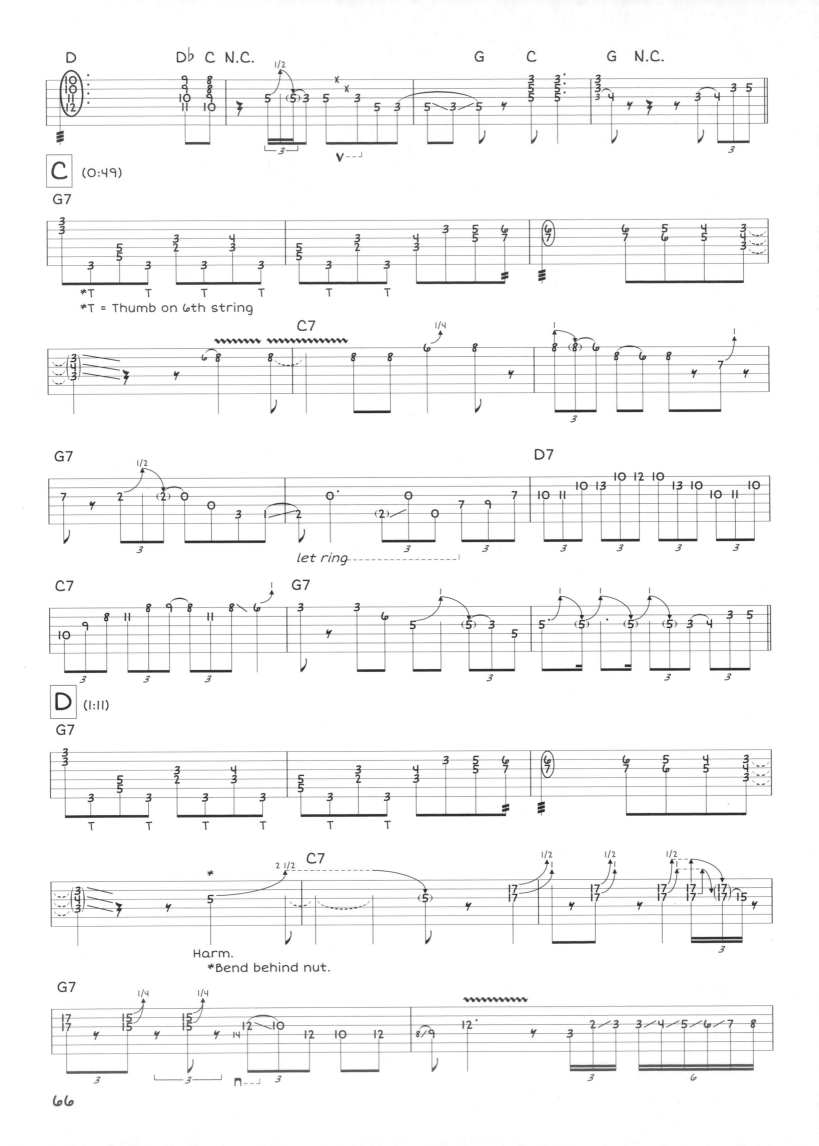

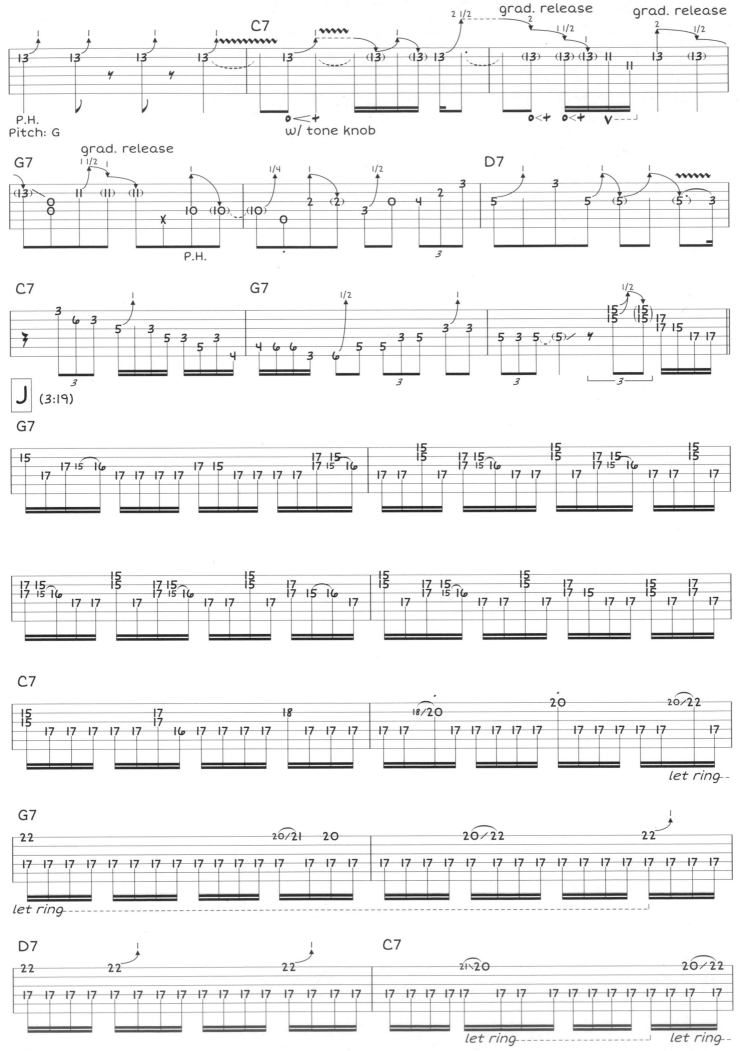

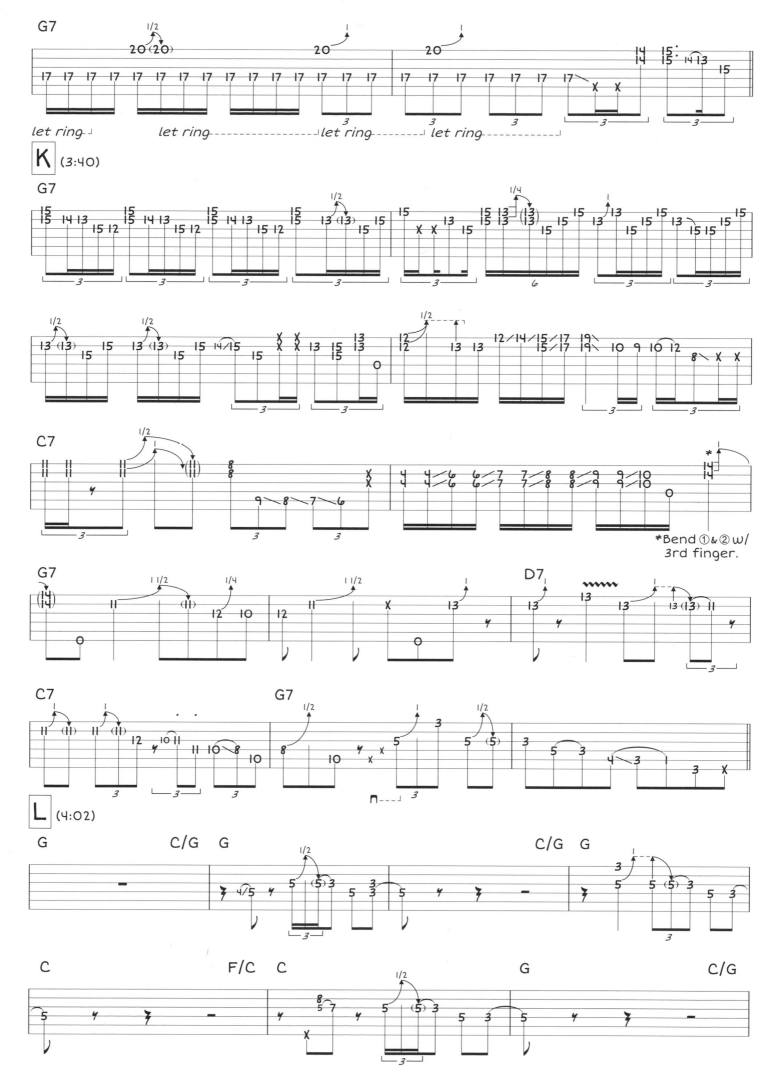

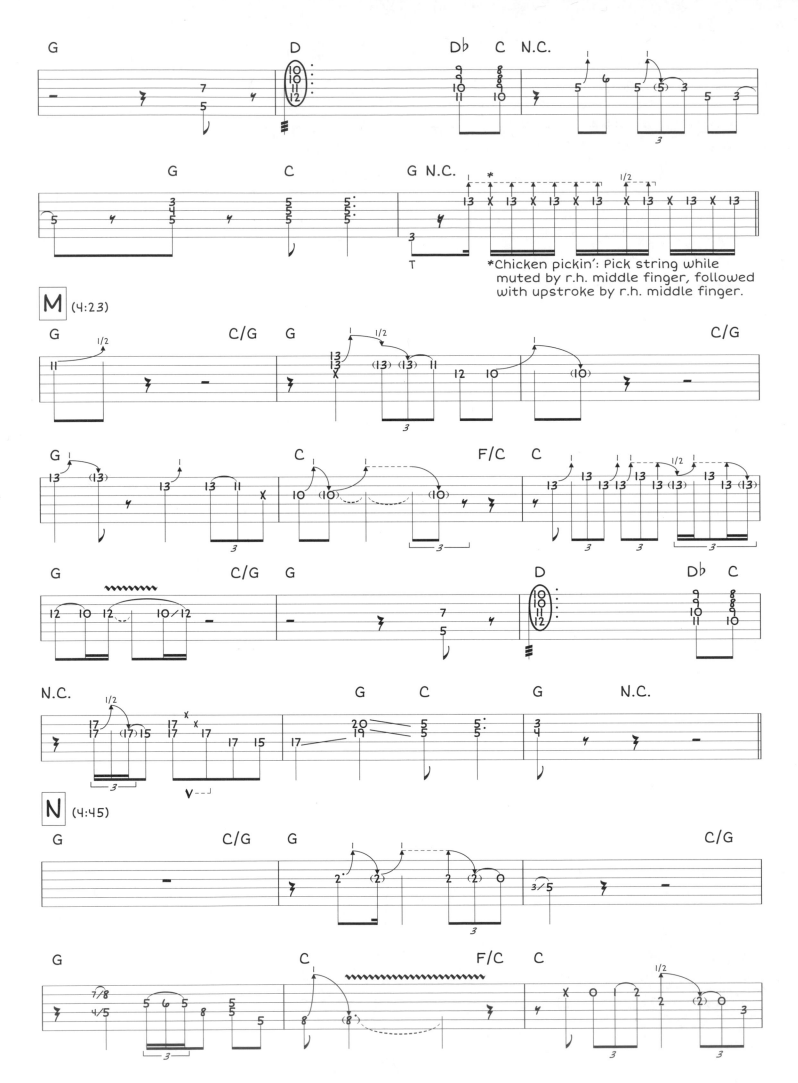

*Chicken pickin': Pick string while muted by r.h. middle finger, followed with upstroke by r.h. middle finger.

M (4:23)

N (4:45)

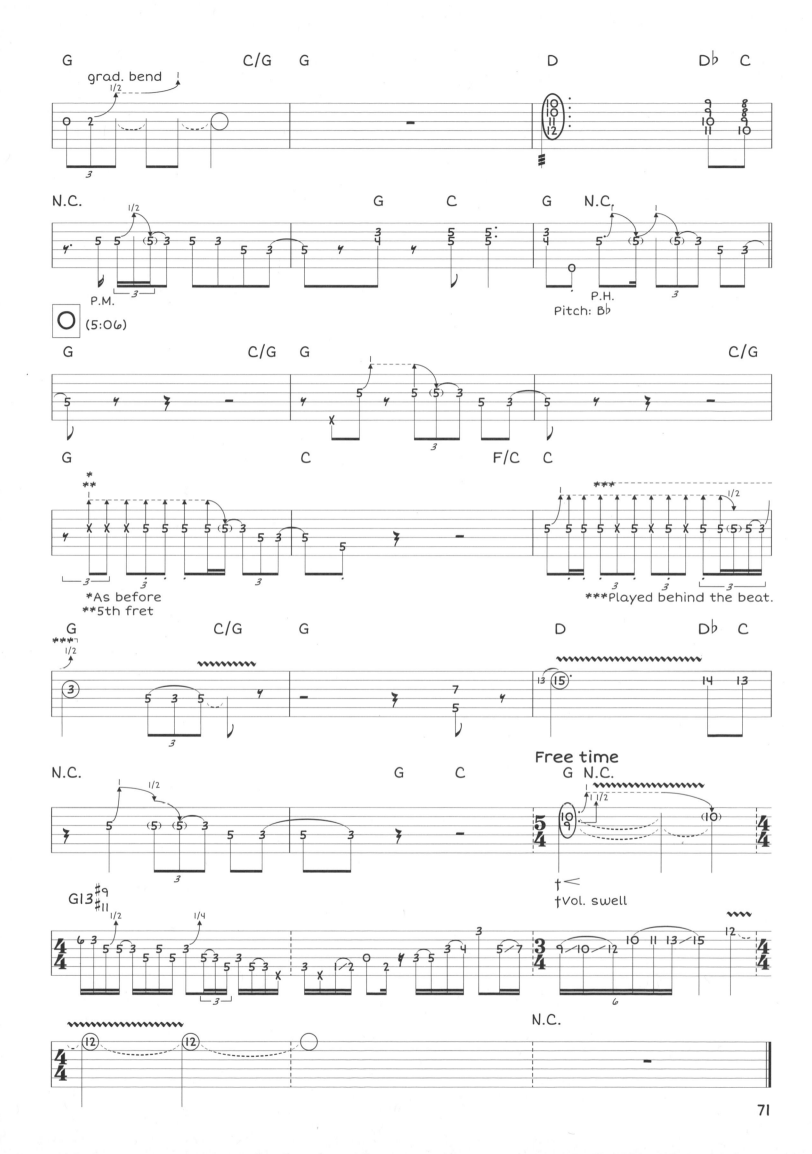

Guitars, Cadillacs

Words and Music by Dwight Yoakam

Guitar: Pete Anderson

Key of A

Intro

Fast (♫ = ♪♪)

N.C.

w/ clean tone

A

Verse

Girl, you taught me how to hurt

A	A	E	E
E	E	A	A
A	A	E	E
E	E	A	E

Chorus

Now it's   guitars,

A	A	E	E
E	E	A	E
A	A	E	E
E	E	A	A

Guitar Solo 1

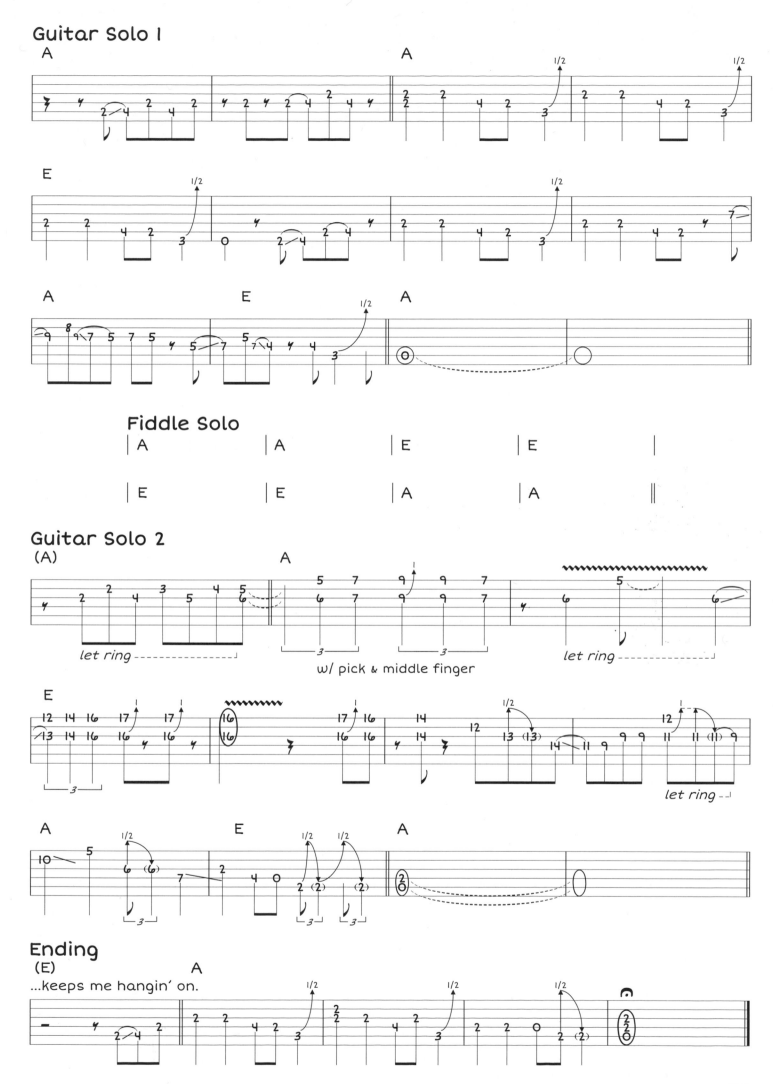

Fiddle Solo

| A | A | E | E | |
| E | E | A | A | ‖ |

Guitar Solo 2

Ending

...keeps me hangin' on.

from Travis Tritt - *It's All About to Change*

Here's a Quarter
(Call Someone Who Cares)

Words and Music by Travis Tritt

**Guitar: Travis Tritt,
Wendell Cox, Richard Bennett**

Key of G

Intro

Moderately

G
(acous.)

let ring --------------- *sim.*

Verse

You say you were   wrong

G	G	C	G	
G	G	D	D	
G	G	C	G	
G	D	G	G	

Chorus

Call someone who'll   listen

C	C	G	G	
G	G	D	D	
G	G7/B	C	G	
G	D	G	G	

*Guitar Solo

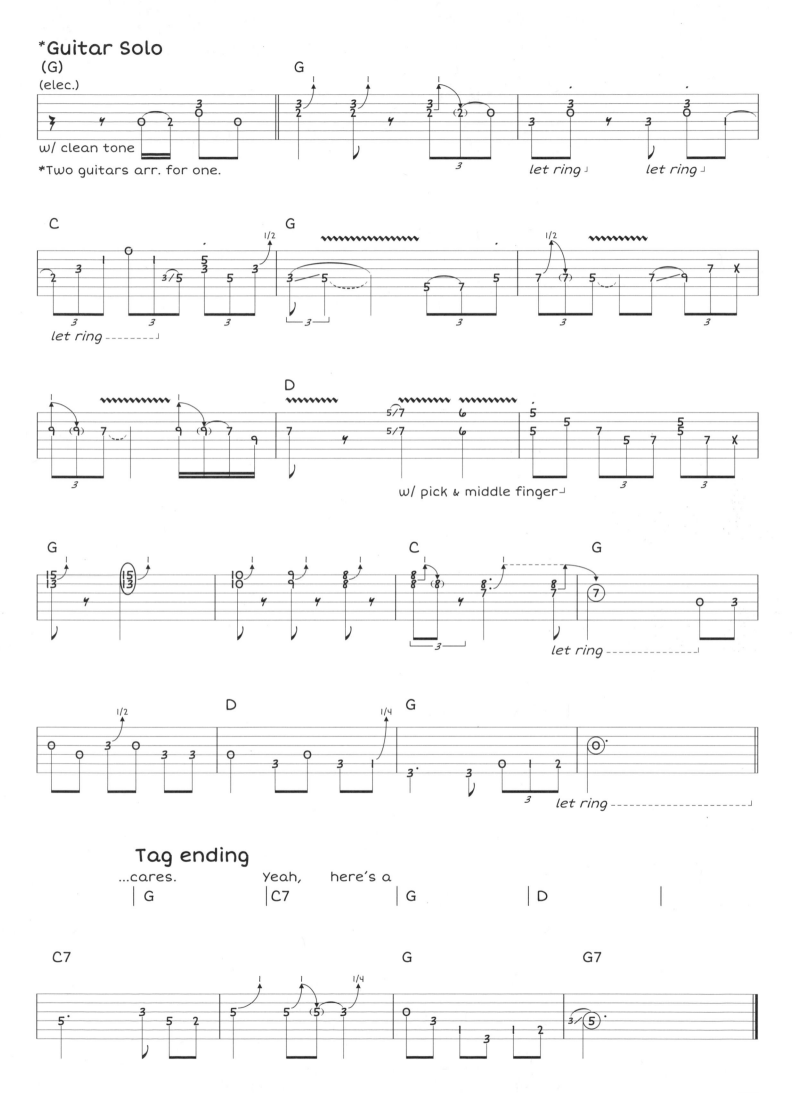

Tag ending

...cares.   Yeah,   here's a
| G | C7 | G | D | |

Highlander Boogie

Words and Music by John Jorgenson

Guitar: John Jorgenson,
Will Ray, Jerry Donahue

Key of A

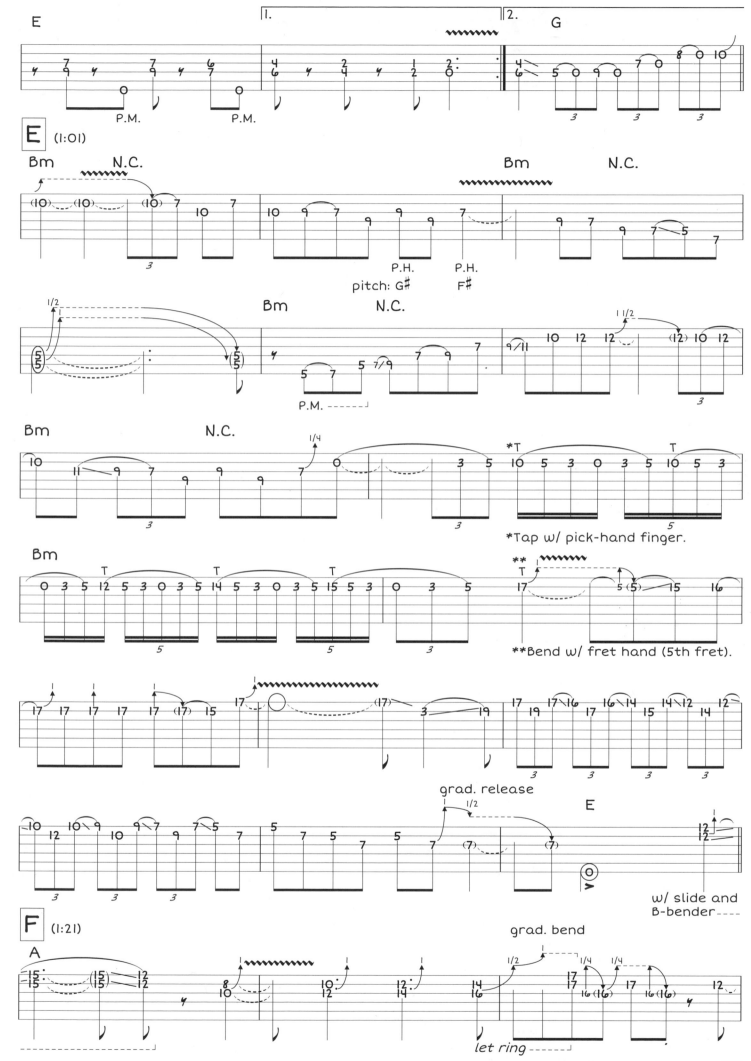

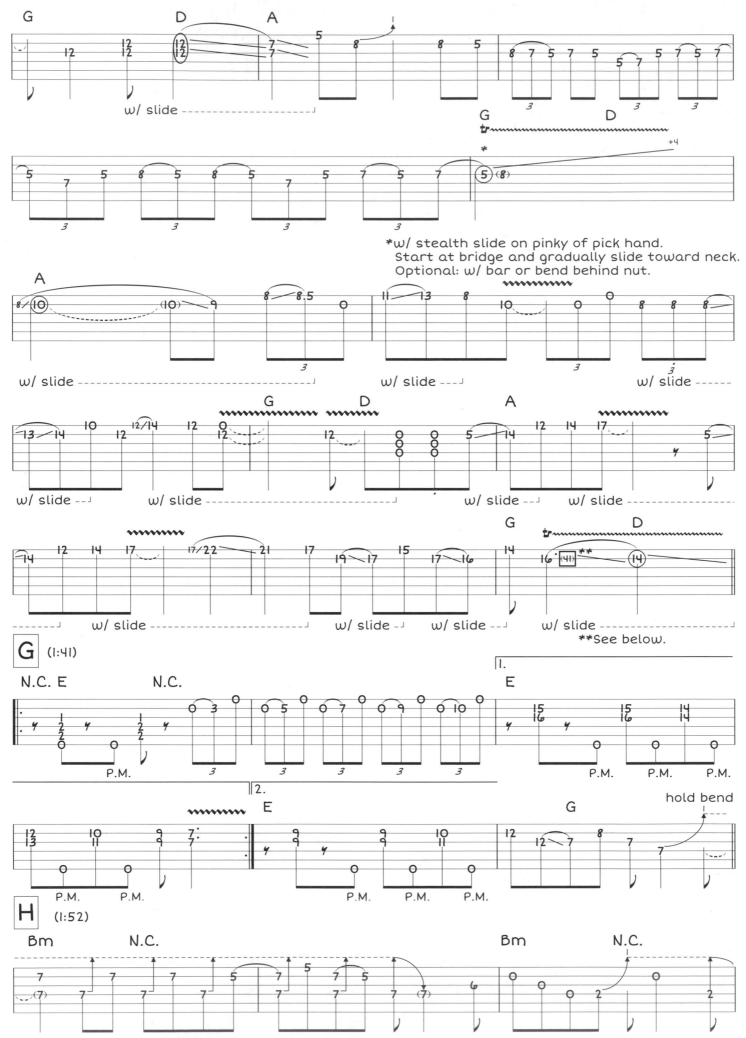

*w/ stealth slide on pinky of pick hand.
Start at bridge and gradually slide toward neck.
Optional: w/ bar or bend behind nut.

**See below.

**Hypothetical fret location (approx. over bridge pickup). Pick-hand slide bounces rapidly on string,
producing a trill effect, while fret-hand slide gradually moves down neck.

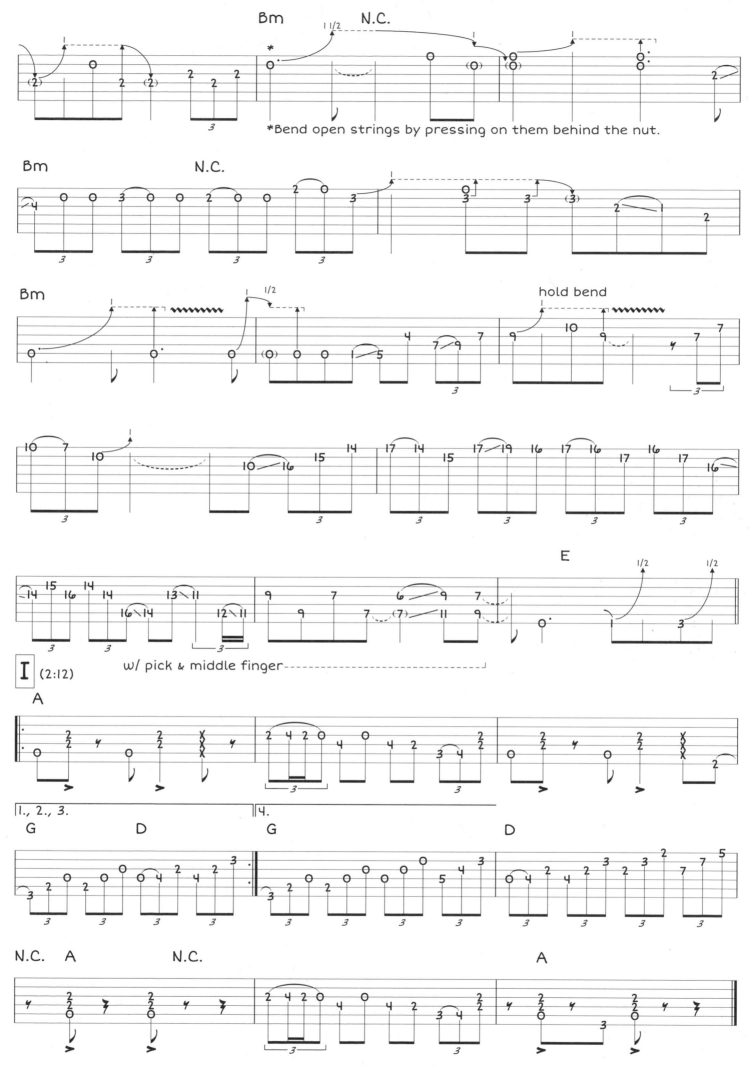

*Bend open strings by pressing on them behind the nut.

w/ pick & middle finger

Highway Patrol

Words and Music by Red Simpson, Dennis Payne and Ray Rush

Guitar: Junior Brown

Key of A

Intro

Fast

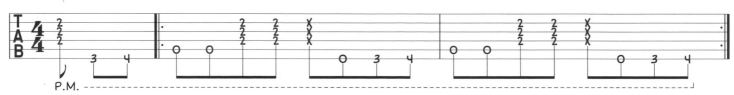

Verse

I got a

A	A	A	A	
D7	D7	A	A	
E	E	A N.C.		

Interlude

Interlude

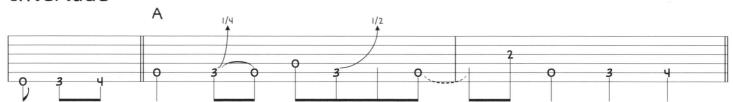

Bridge

On the Highway Patrol

D7	D7	A	A	
D7	D7	A N.C.		

Guitar Solo

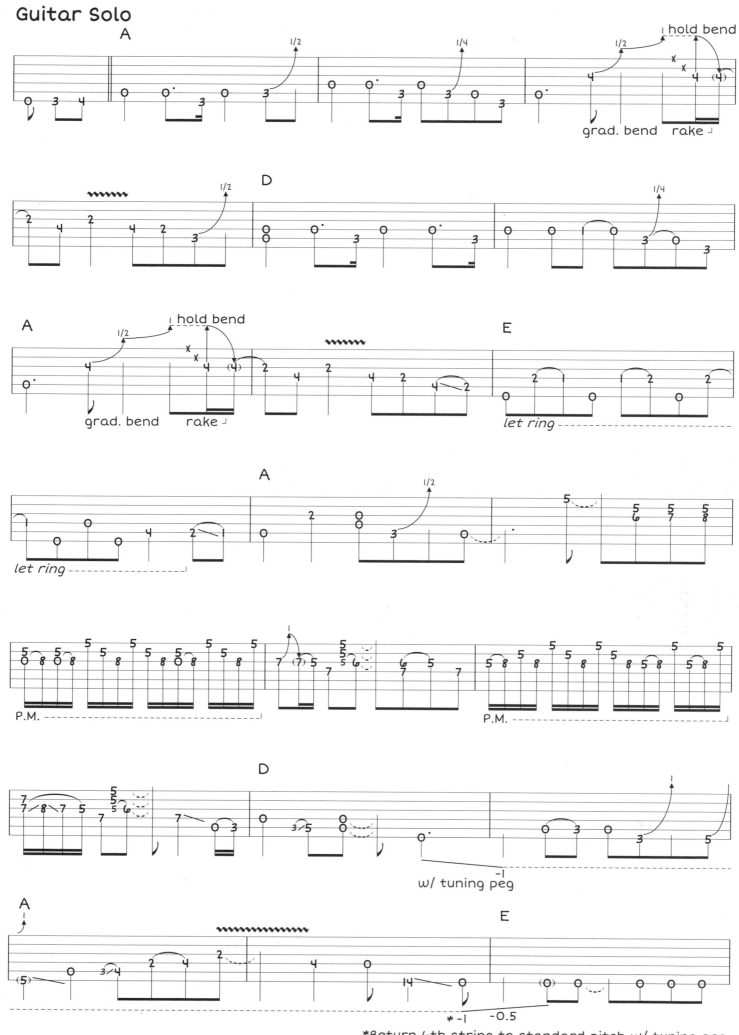

*Return 6th string to standard pitch w/ tuning peg.

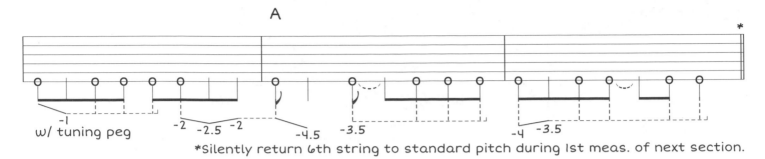

*Silently return 6th string to standard pitch during 1st meas. of next section.

Ending

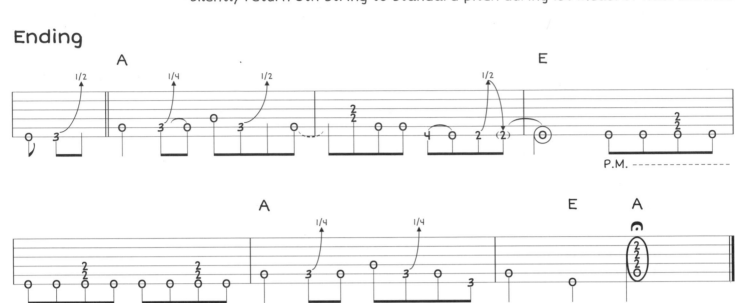

from Blake Shelton - *Hillbilly Bone*

Hillbilly Bone

Words and Music by Luke Laird and Craig Wiseman

Guitar: Tom Bukovac

Key of G

Intro

Moderately slow

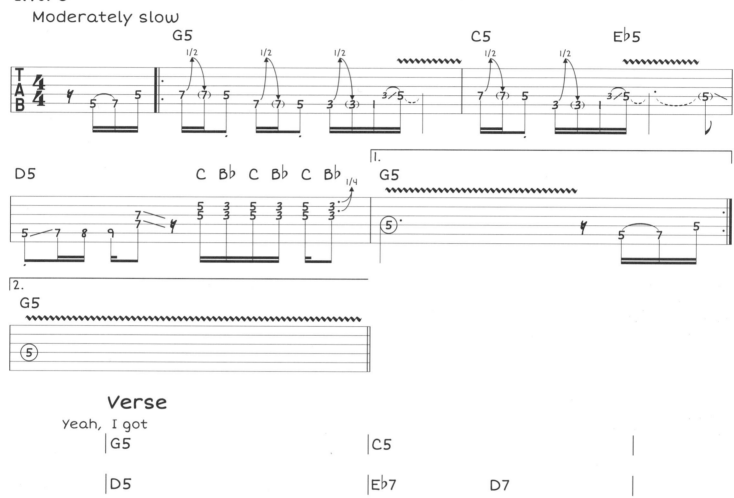

Verse

Yeah, I got

	G5		C5	
|D5	|Eb7	D7	
	G5		C5	
	D5		Eb7	C Bb C Bb C Bb ‖

Chorus

We all got a hillbilly bone

	G5		C5	
|D5	|Fsus2	C Bb C Bb C Bb	
	G5		C5	
	D5		G5	N.C. ‖

83

Interlude

w/ Intro riff

|G5 |C5   Eb5 |

|D5   C Bb C Bb C Bb |G5   ‖

Verse

Now, you ain't

|G5 |C5   N.C. |

|D5 |Eb7   D7 |

|G5 |C5 |

|D5 |Eb7 |

|D7   D7#9   ‖

Guitar Solo

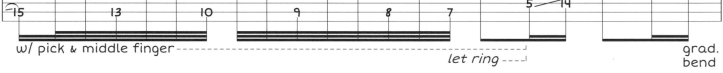

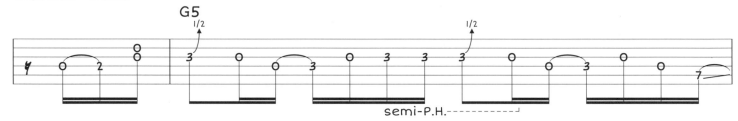

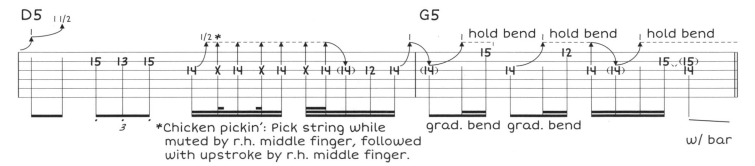

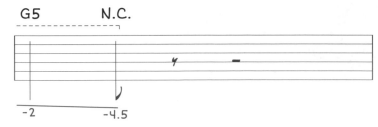

Chorus

We all got a hillbilly bone

|G5 N.C.			
		F5 C5 N.C. C5 B♭5	
|G5	|C5	
|D5	|G5 N.C.	
|G5 N.C.	|G5 N.C.	
|G5 N.C.	‖

Outro

w/ Intro riff

Hollywood Boogie

Words and Music by Harry Stinson, Kenny Vaughan, Marty Stuart and Paul Martin

Guitar: Kenny Vaughan, Marty Stuart

Key of A

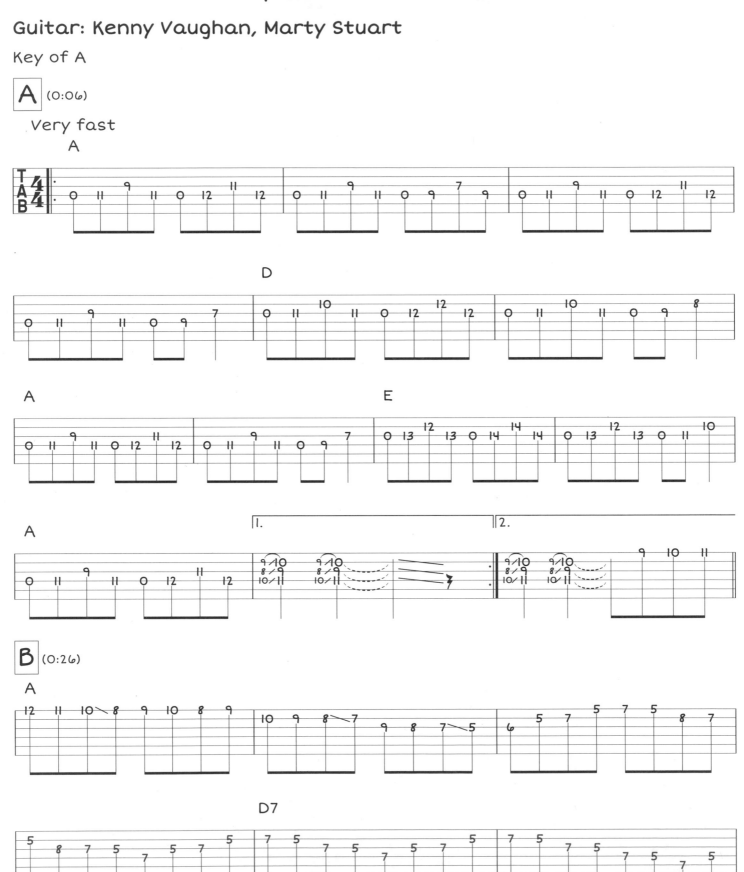

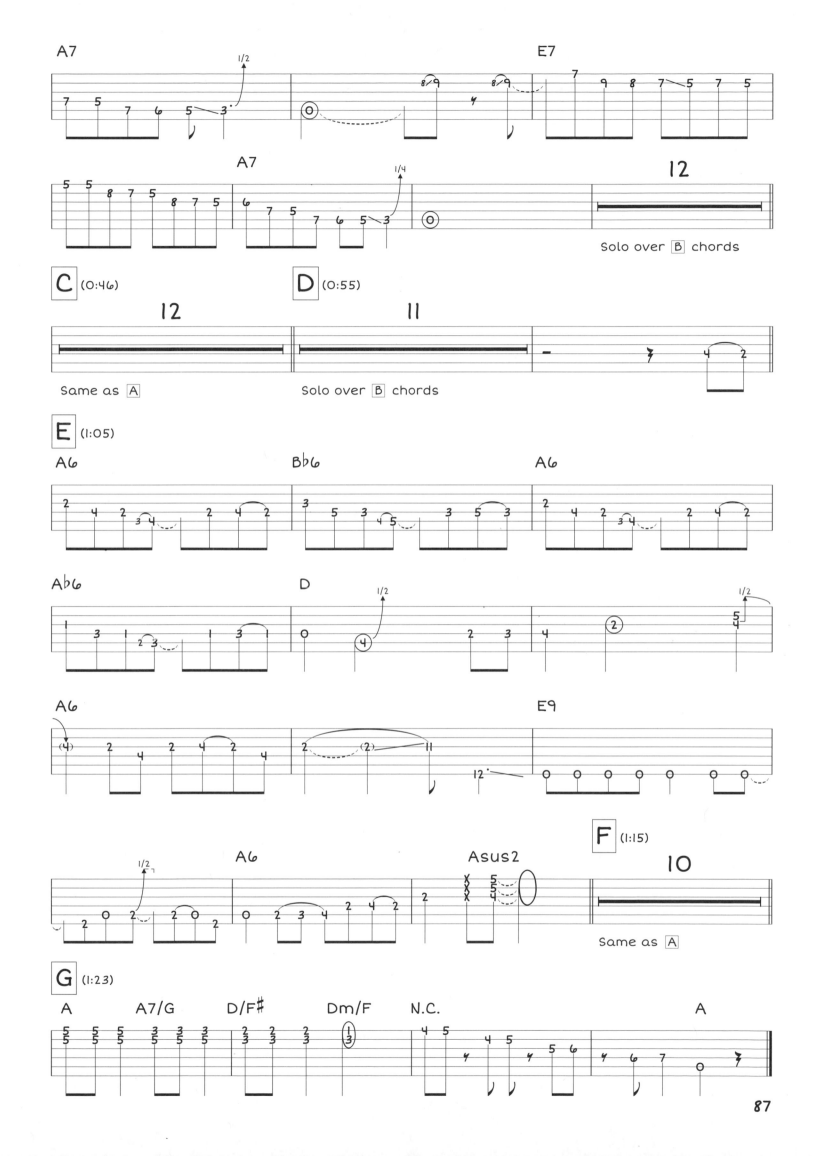

from Toby Keith - *How Do You Like Me Now?!*

How Do You Like Me Now?!

Words and Music by Toby Keith and Chuck Cannon

Guitar: Brent Mason

Key of C

Intro

Moderately

w/ clean tone

let ring

let ring

let ring   let ring

Verse

Yeah, I was always the crazy one,

| G | | F | | |

| G | | F | C | |

| G7 | | C | F | |

| G7 | | C | G   N.C. ‖

Pre-Chorus

w/ Intro riff

How do you like me now?

| C   F/C | C ‖

Chorus

How do you like me now,

| F | C | G | C |

Omit 1st time

| F | C | G | C ‖

Interlude

w/ Intro riff

| C F/C | | C C6sus2 C | | F/C | | C C6sus2 C ‖

Guitar Solo

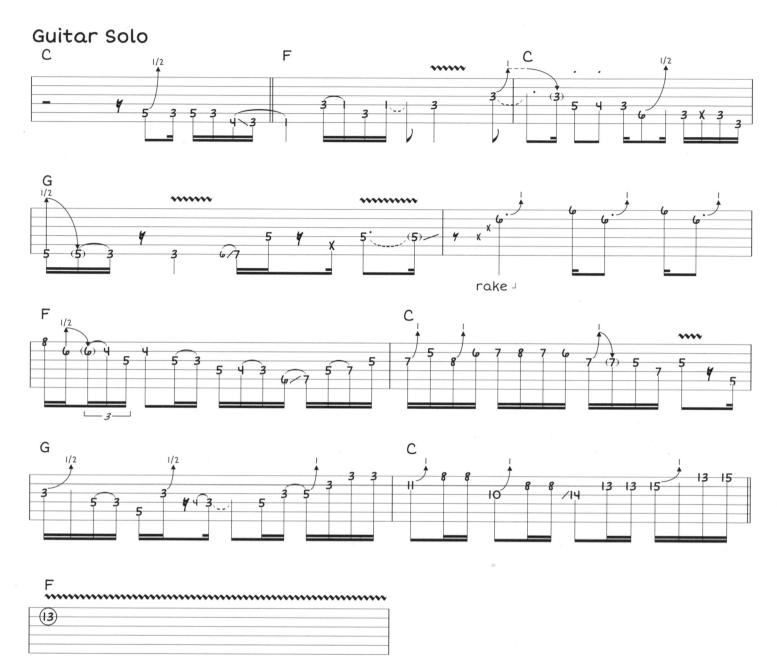

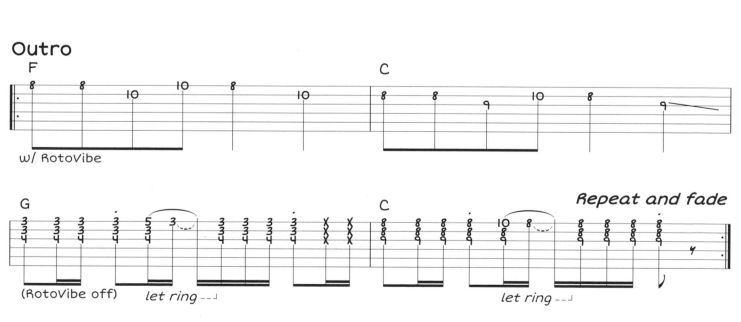

Outro

F

w/ RotoVibe

C

G

(RotoVibe off)   *let ring*

C

Repeat and fade

let ring

from Merle Haggard - *Back to the Barrooms*

I Think I'll Just
Stay Here and Drink
Words and Music by Merle Haggard

Guitar: Reggie Young, Merle Haggard

Key of A

Verse

Moderately

I could be holding you tonight,

| 4/4 A5 | | ‖D7 | |D7 | |A7 | |

| |A7 | |E7 | |E7 | |A7 | |

| |A7 | ‖ |

Guitar Solo I

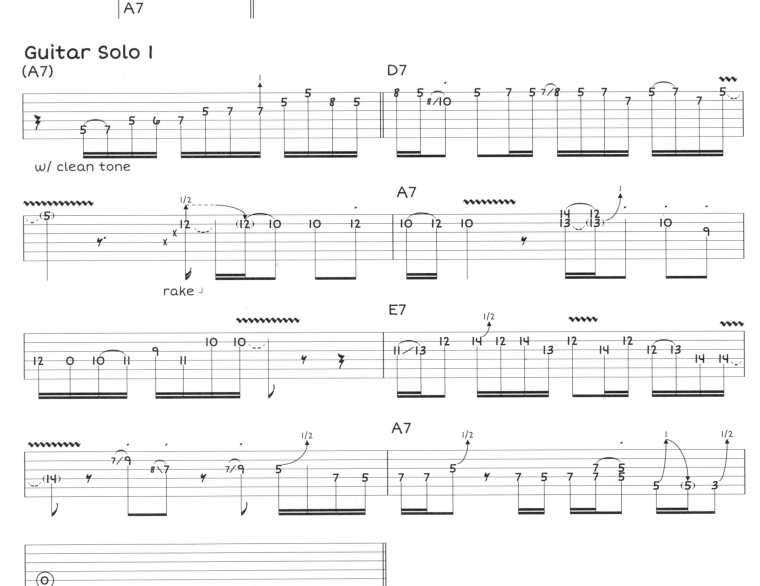

Piano Solo
w/ Verse pattern

Guitar Solo 2

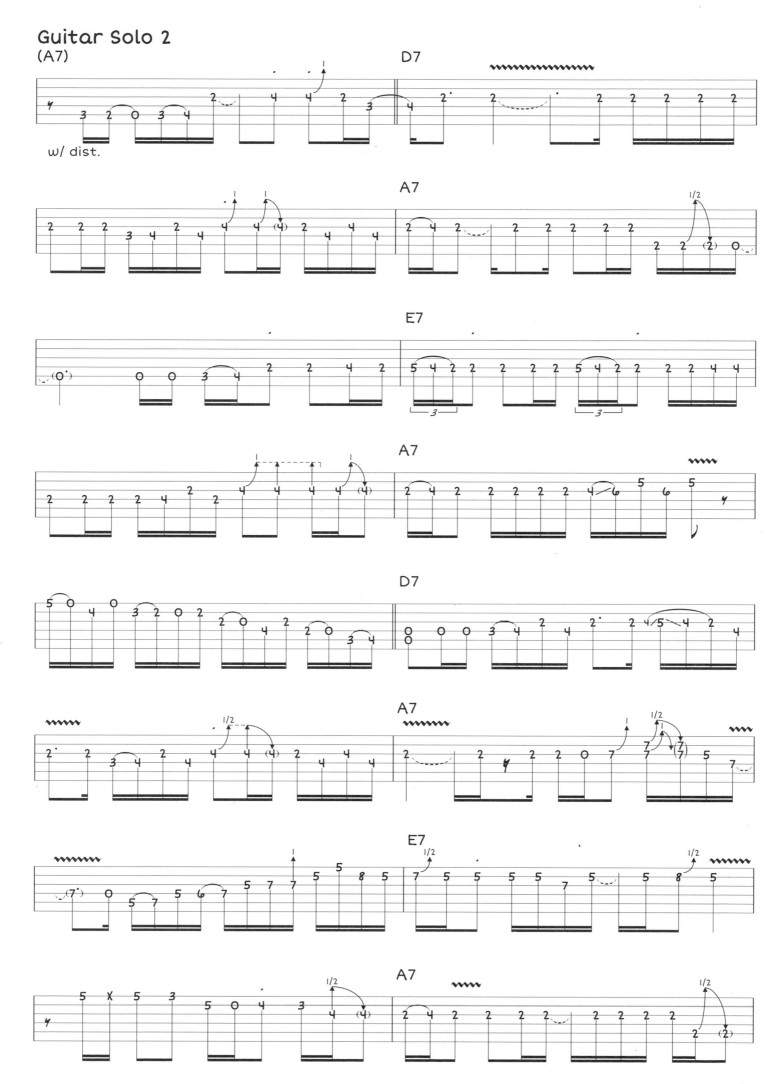

Sax Solo
w/ Verse pattern

Guitar Solo 3

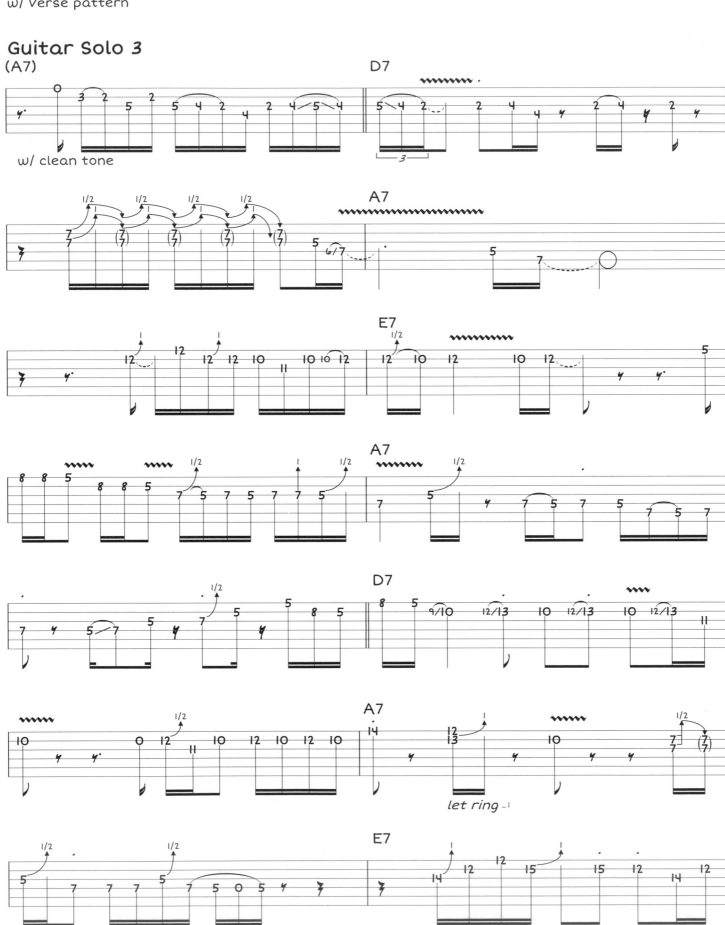

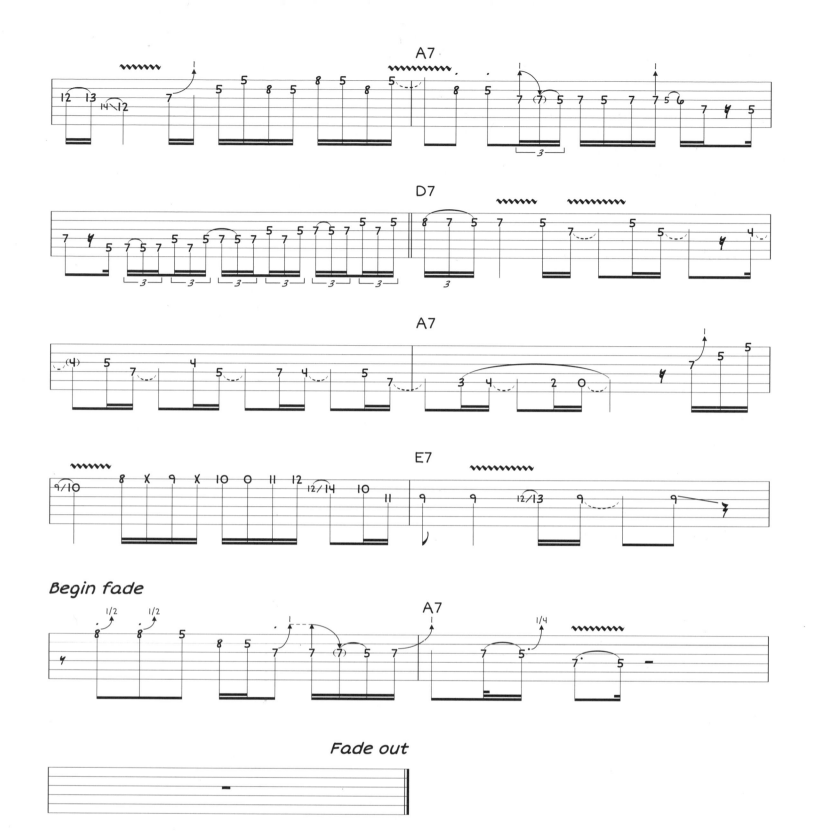

Jerry's Breakdown

By Jerry Reed

Guitar: Jerry Reed, Chet Atkins

Key of E

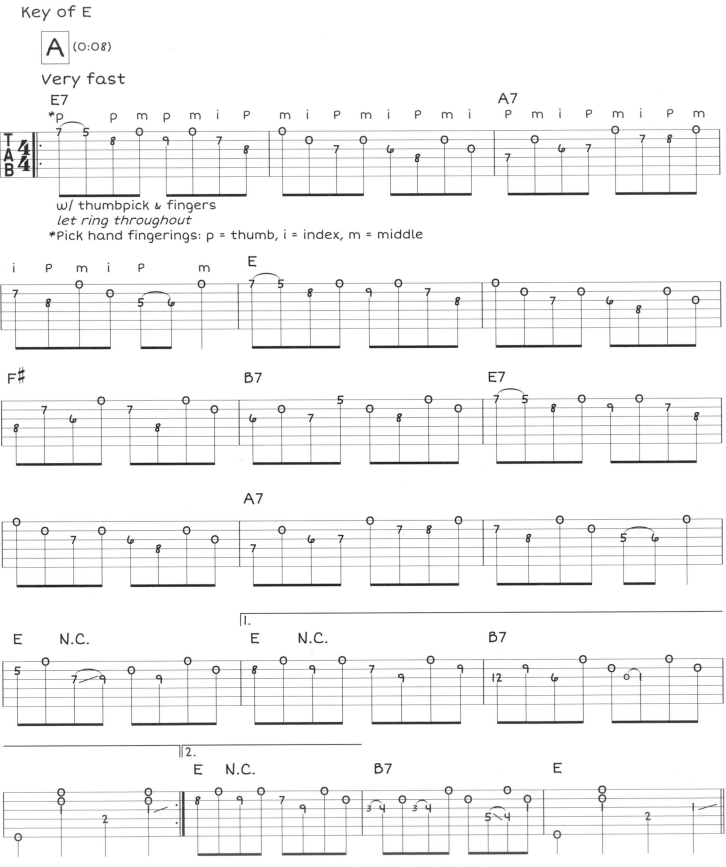

w/ thumbpick & fingers
let ring throughout
*Pick hand fingerings: p = thumb, i = index, m = middle

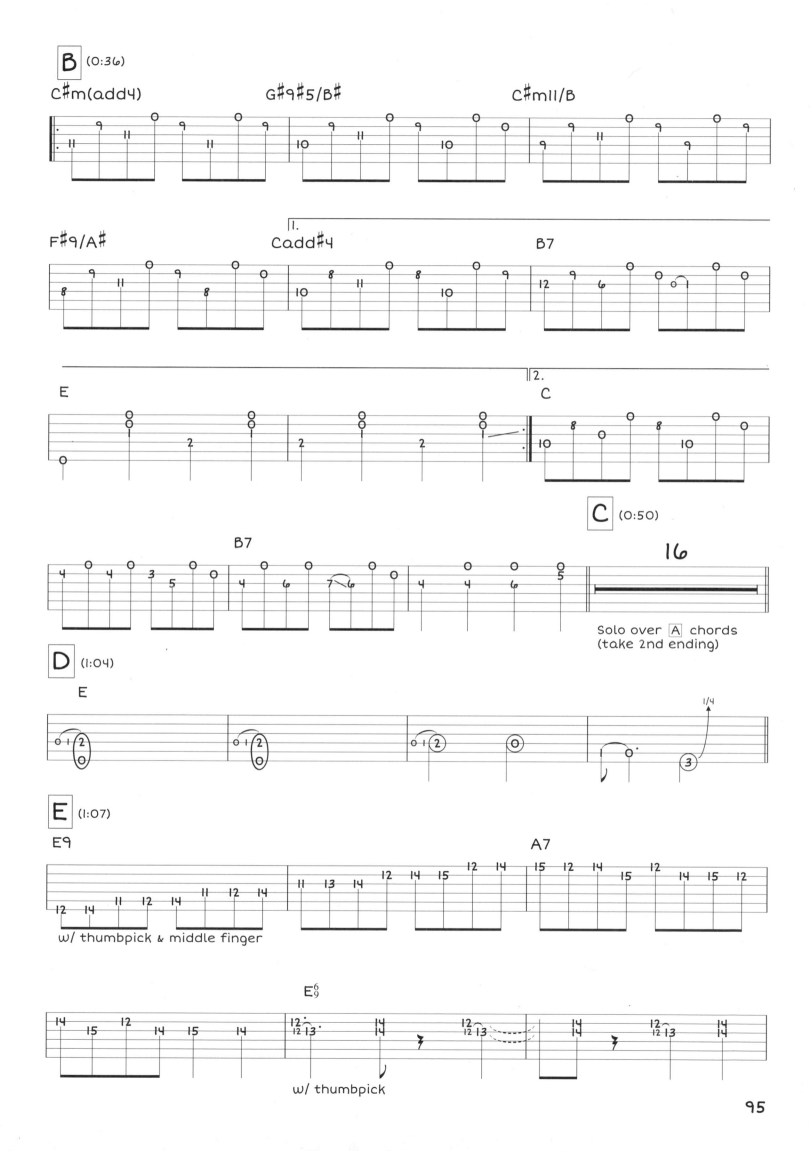

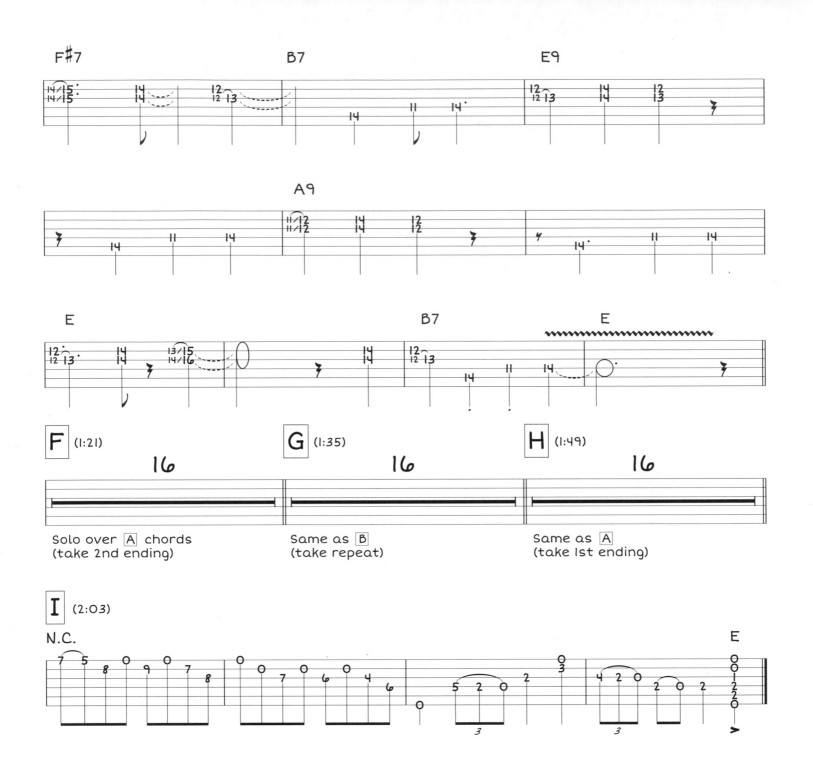

F (1:21)

16

Solo over A chords
(take 2nd ending)

G (1:35)

16

Same as B
(take repeat)

H (1:49)

16

Same as A
(take 1st ending)

I (2:03)

N.C.

from Vince Gill - *Pocket Full of Gold*

Liza Jane

Words and Music by Vincent Gill and Reed Nielsen

Guitar: Vince Gill

Key of A

Intro

Very fast

N.C. A5

*T = Thumb on 6th string

Verse

You've   got my number.

|A5 |A5 |A5 |A5 |

|A5 |A5 |A5 |A5 |

|C5 |C5 |D5 |D5   ‖

Interlude

w/ Intro riff

|A5 |A5 |A5 |A5   ‖

Chorus

Girl, I got it   bad

|D5 |A5 |D5 |A5 |

|D5 |A5 |E5 |E5   ‖

Guitar Solo

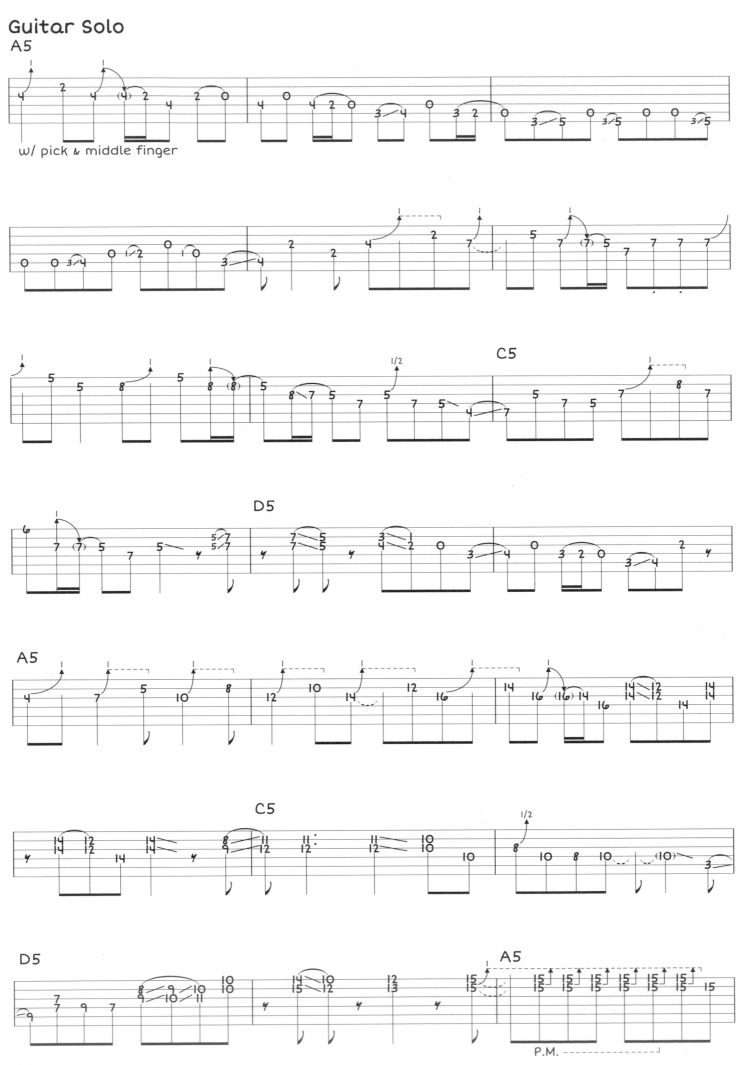

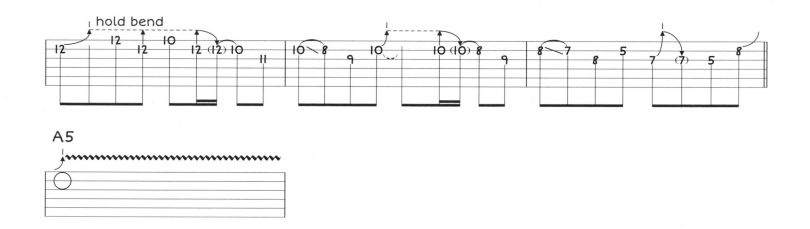

A5

Outro
w/ Intro riff

from George Strait - *Easy Come, Easy Go*

Love Bug

Words and Music by Clarence Kemp and Wayne Curtis

Guitar: Brent Mason

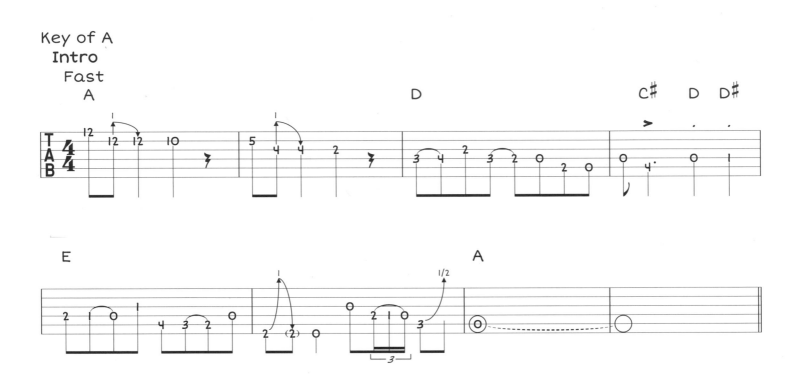

Key of A
Intro
Fast

Verse

Well, I was ruling   the roost

	A		A		E		E	

	E		E		A		A	

	A		A		D		D	

	E		E		A	²⁄₄A N.C.	⁴⁄₄

Oh, that

|⁴⁄₄ | ‖

Chorus

little bitty

A	A	E	E	
E	E	A	A	
A	A	D	D	
E	E	A	A	

Guitar Solo

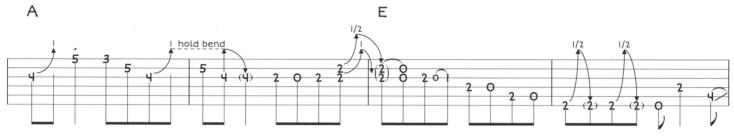

Fiddle Solo

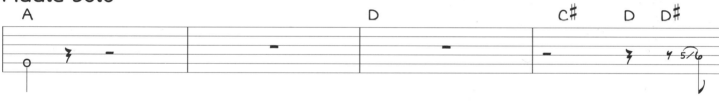

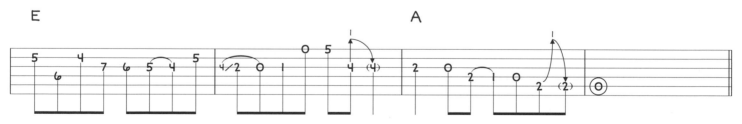

Outro

w/ Intro riff

| A | A | D | C# D D# |
| E | E | |

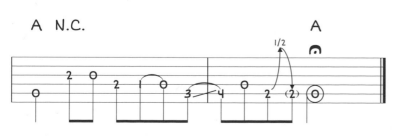

from Rodney Crowell - *Life Is Messy*

Lovin' All Night

Words and Music by Rodney Crowell

Guitar: Kenny Vaughn

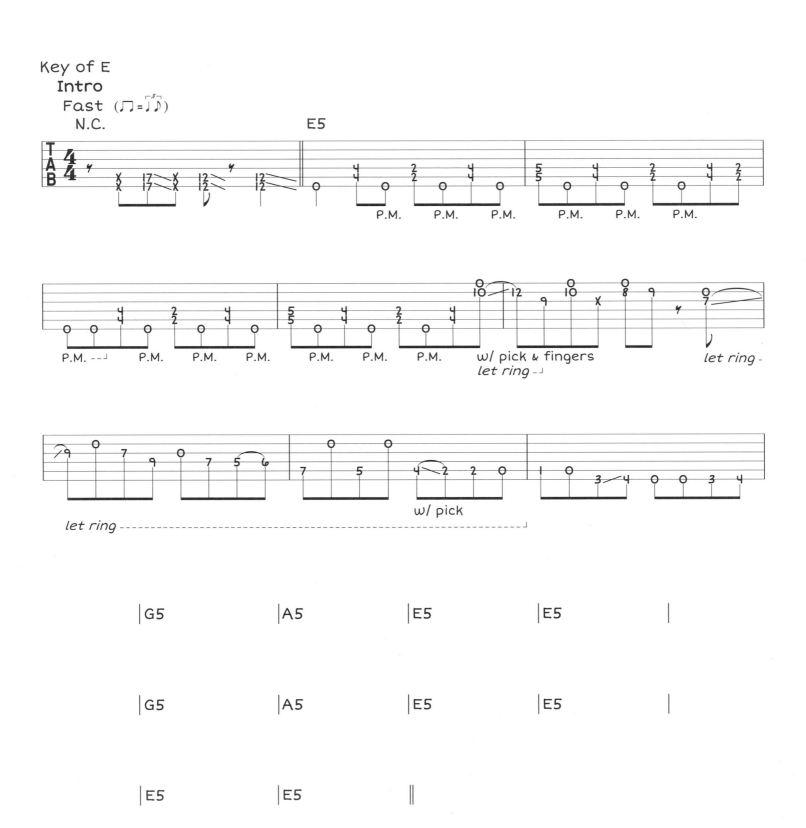

Verse

Now, baby

|E5 |E5 |E5 |E5 |

|E5 |E5 |E5 |E5 |

|E5 |E5 |E5 |E5 |

|E5 |E5 F#5 G5 G#5 ‖

Chorus

We've been lovin' all night

|A5 |G5 |E5 |E5 |

|A5 |G5 |E5 |E5 |

|D5 |D5 |E5 |E5   ‖

Interlude

w/ Intro riff

|E5 |E5 |E5 |E5   ‖

Guitar Solo

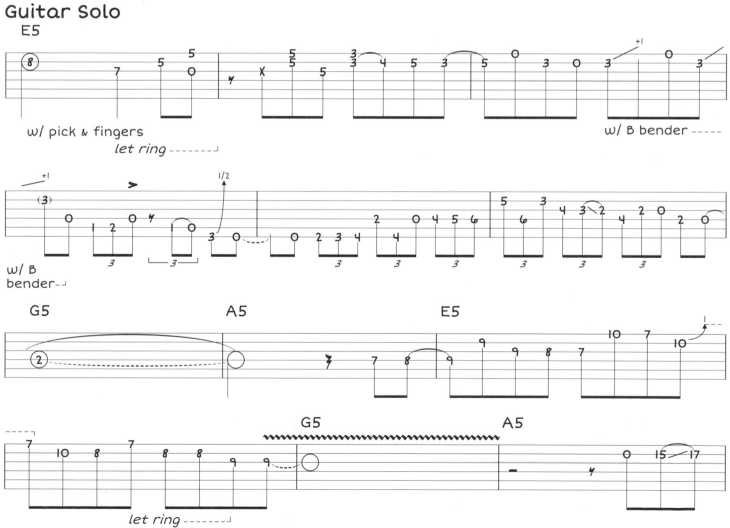

E5

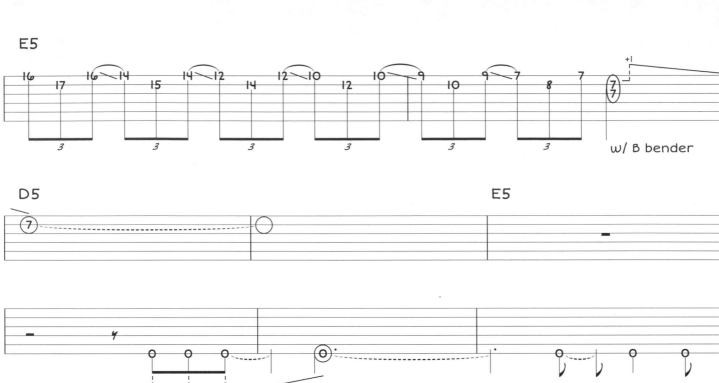

w/ B bender

D5   E5

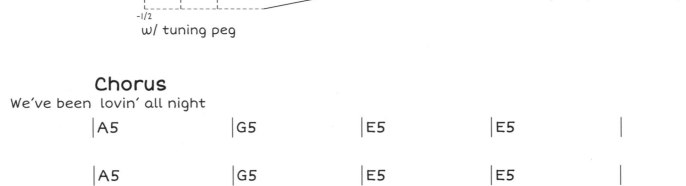

-1/2

w/ tuning peg

Chorus
We've been lovin' all night

|A5 |G5 |E5 |E5 |

|A5 |G5 |E5 |E5 |

|D5 |D5 |E5   D5 |C#5   B5 |

|D5 |D5 |E5 |E5   ‖

Interlude
w/ Intro riff

|E5 |E5 |E5 |E5   ‖

Outro
Been lovin' all night

‖: G5 |G5 |A5 |A5 |

1., 2.
|E5 |E5   :‖

3.

E5

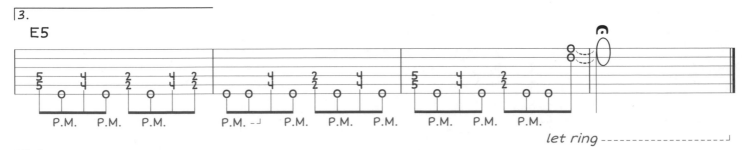

P.M.   P.M.   P.M.   P.M.   P.M.   P.M.   P.M.   P.M.   P.M.   P.M.

let ring

from Diamond Rio - *Close to the Edge*

Oh Me, Oh My Sweet Baby

Words and Music by Michael Garvin and Tom Shapiro

Guitar: Jimmy Olander

Key of C

Intro

Fast

N.C.

Chorus

Oh, me,   oh,   my sweet baby

C	C	G	G
G	G	C	C G
C	C	G	G
G	G	C	C

Verse

I remember how she'd

F	F	C	C
G	G	C	C
F	F	C	C
F F# G F	F# G F F#	G F	C/E G/D

Guitar Solo

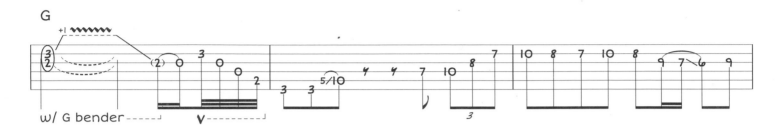

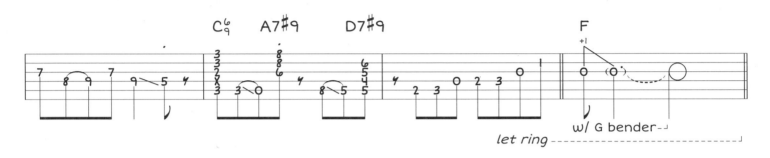

Breakdown-Chorus

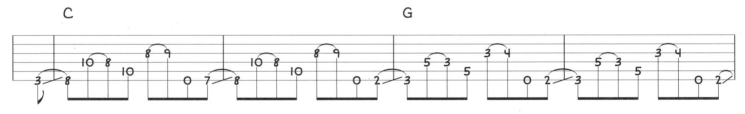

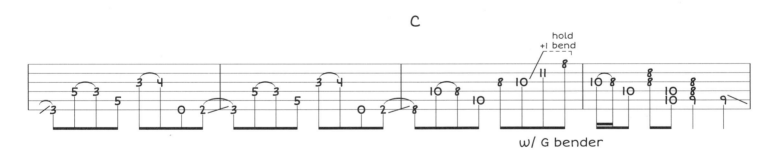

|C |C |G |G |

|G |G |N.C. C$_9^6$ |C$_9^6$ ||

Outro

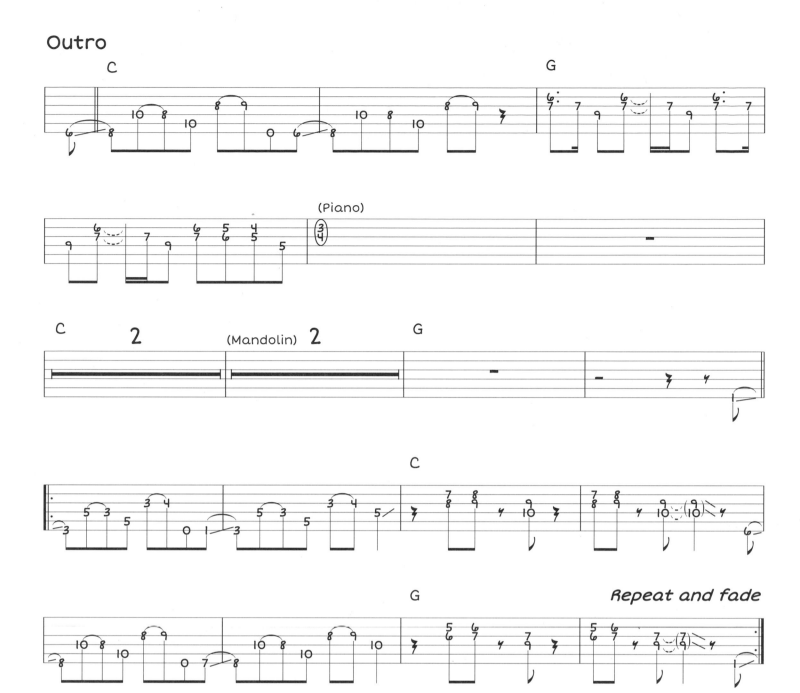

Move It on Over
Words and Music by Hank Williams

Guitar: Zeke Turner

Key of E

Intro
Fast (♫ = ♪♪)

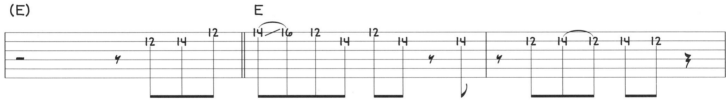

Verse
Came in last night at half past ten.

E	E	E	E7	
A	A	E	E	
B7	B7	E	E	

Guitar Solo
(E)

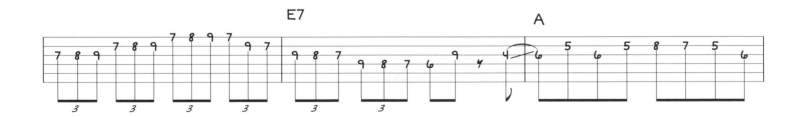

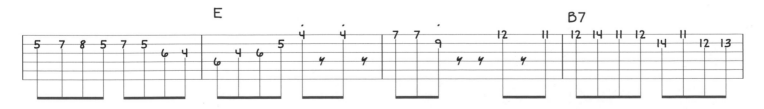

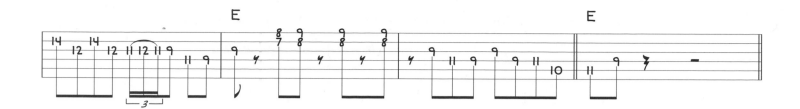

Pedal Steel Solo
w/ Verse pattern

Verse
Remember, pup

|　E　　　　　|　E　　　　　|　E　　　　　|　E7　　　　　|

|　A　　　　　|　A　　　　　|　E　　　　　|　E　　　　　|

|　B7　　　　|　B7　　　　|　E　　　　　|　E　　E6　　‖

The Night Rider

Words and Music by Jim Bryant

Guitar: Jimmy Bryant

Key of Bb

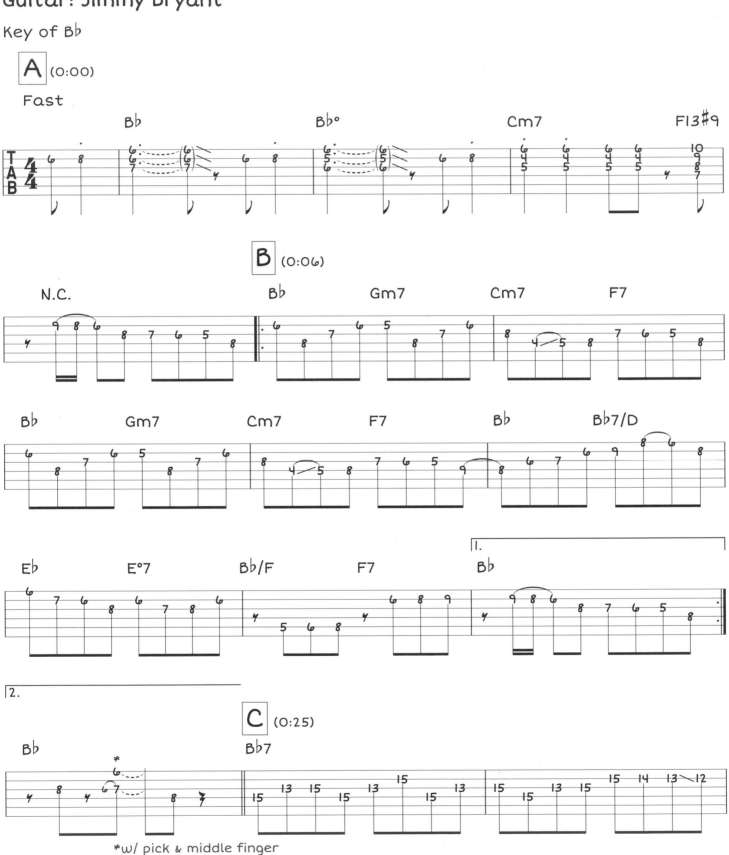

*w/ pick & middle finger

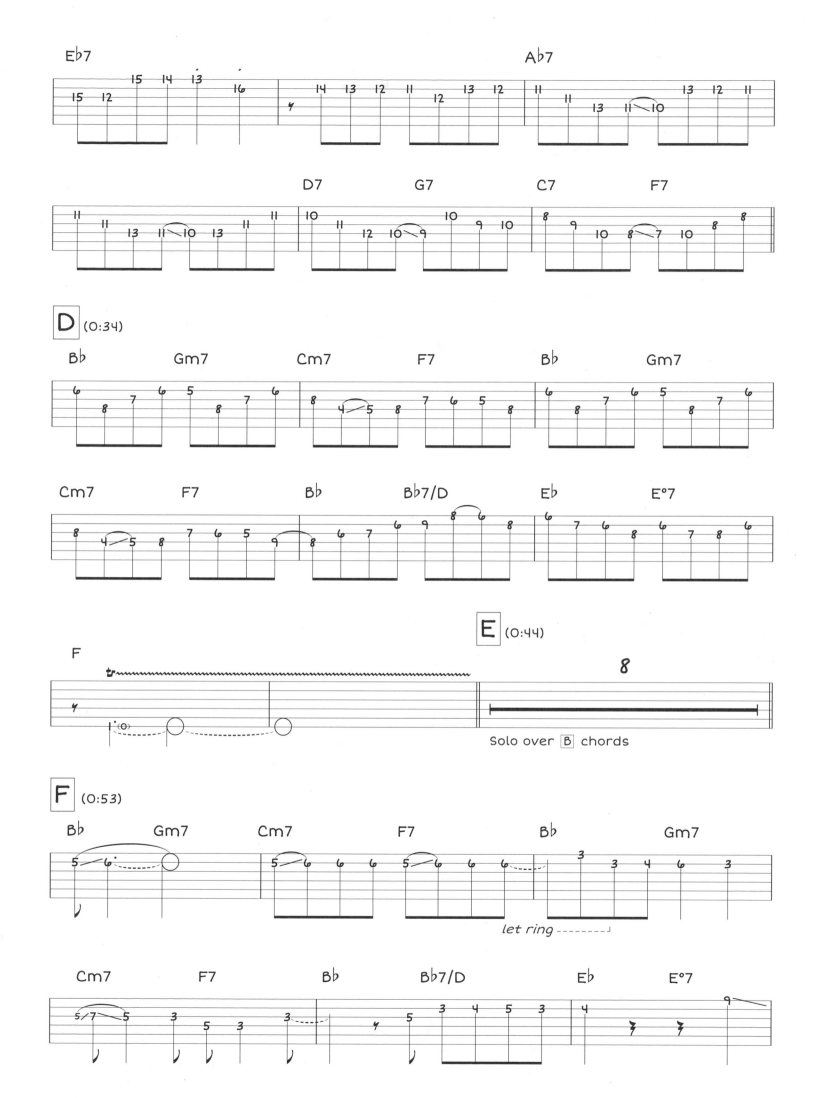

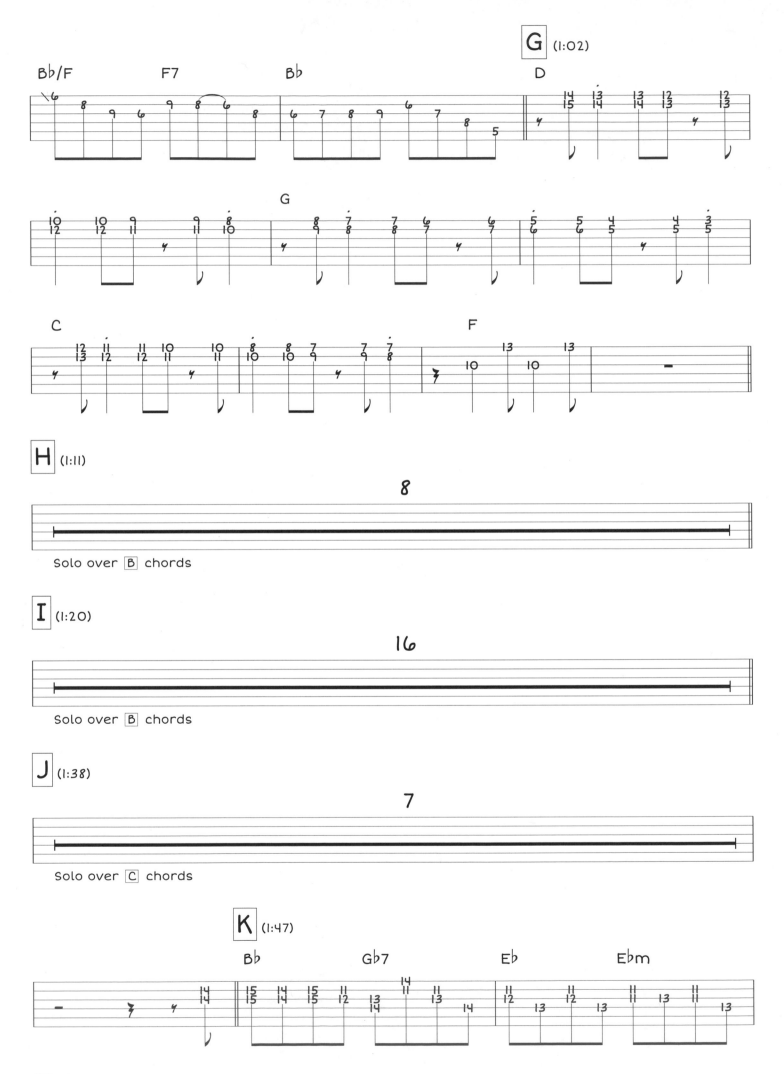

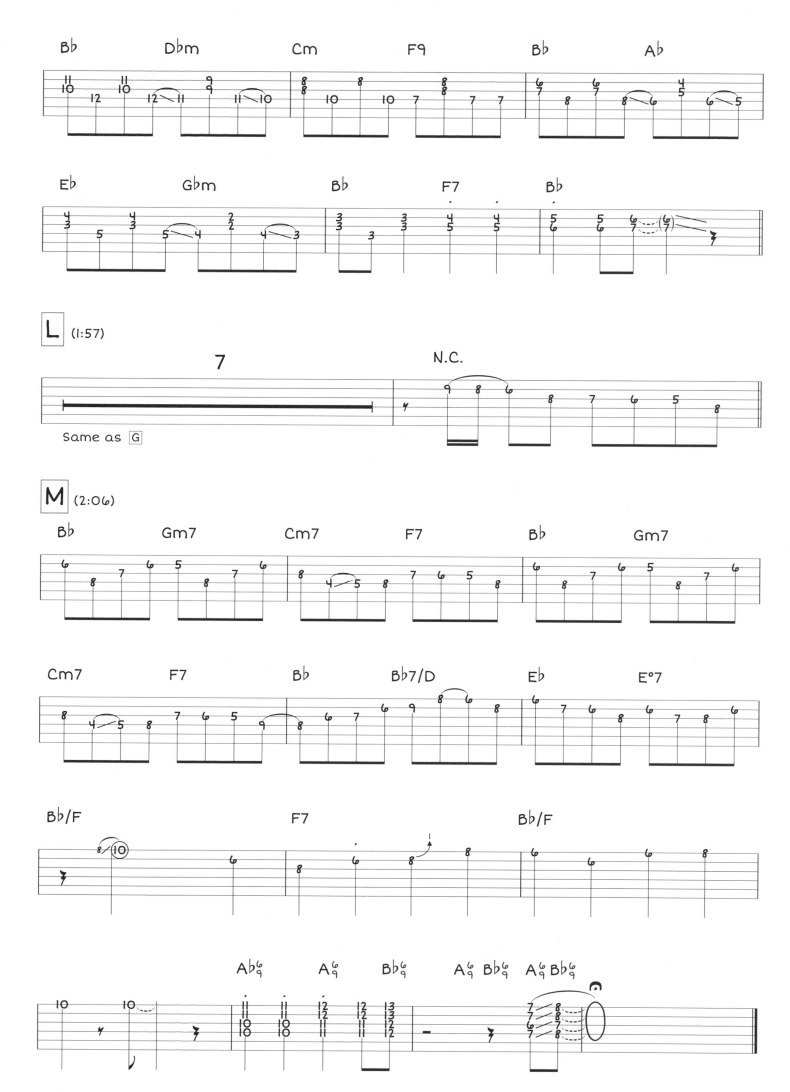

Old Enough to Know Better

Words and Music by Wade Hayes and Chick Rains

Guitar: Brent Mason

Key of B
Intro
Fast

$\frac{4}{4}$ N.C.				

B5				A5 A#5 ‖

Verse

Neon lights

B5	B5	E5	E5	
B5	B5	F#5	F#5	
B5	B5	E5	E5	
B5	B5	F#5	B5	
B5	‖			

Chorus

Monday morning

E5	E5	B5	B5	
B5	B5	F#5	F#5	
B5	B5	E5	E5	
B5	B5			

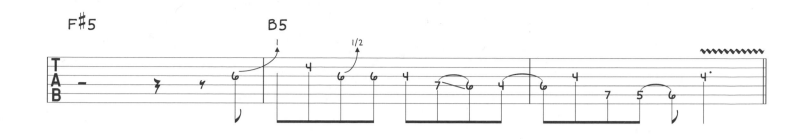

Pedal Steel Solo

| |E5 | |E5 | |B5 | |B5 | |
| |B5 | |B5 | |F#5 | |F#5 | ||

Guitar Solo

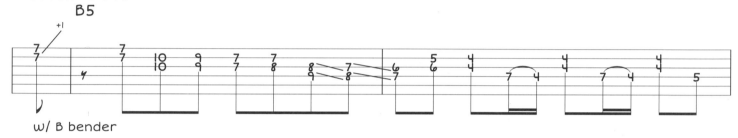

w/ B bender

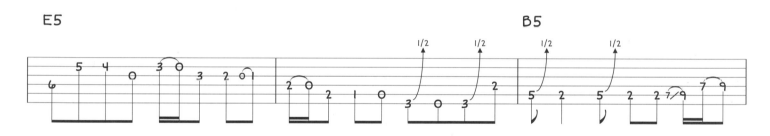

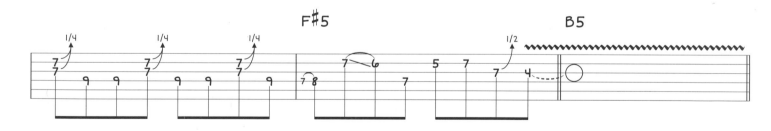

Outro

| | 1., 2., 3. | 4. |
||:B5 | |B5 | |B5 | |E5 | :|| A5 A#5 ||

Repeat & fade

||:B5 | |B5 | |B5 | |E5 | :||

from Johnny Hiland - *Johnny Hiland*

Orange Blossom Special

Words and Music by Ervin T. Rouse

Guitar: Johnny Hiland

Key of A

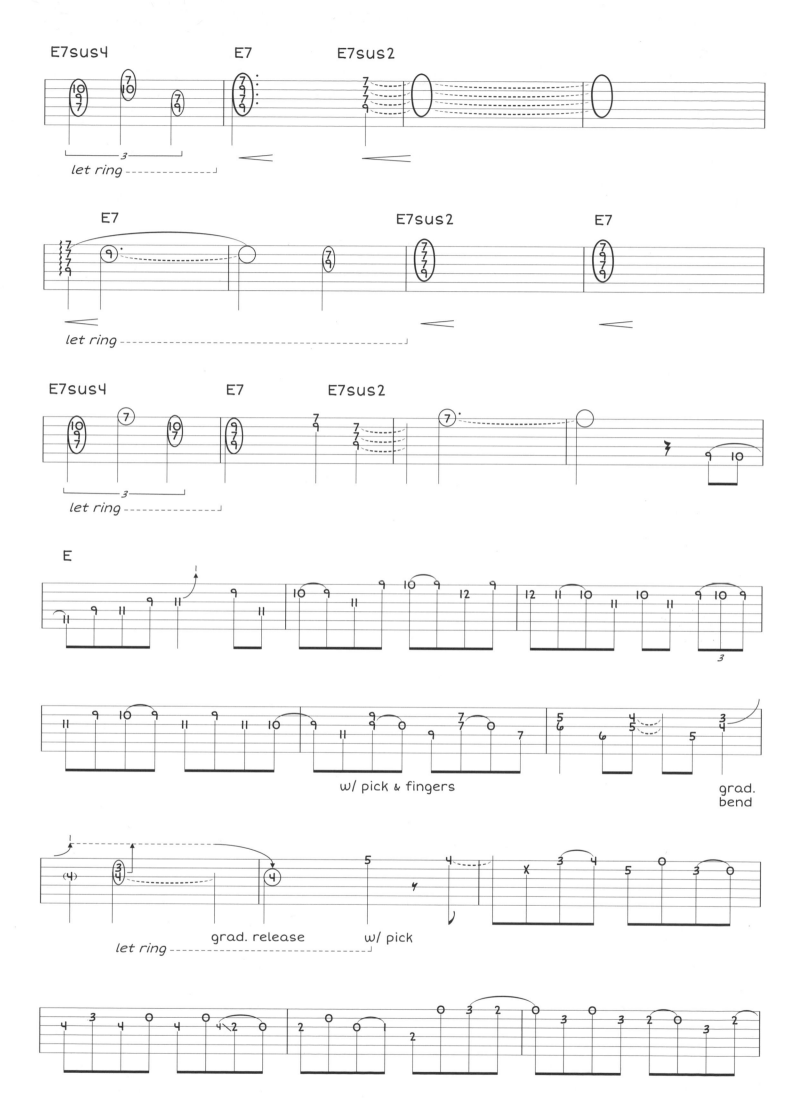

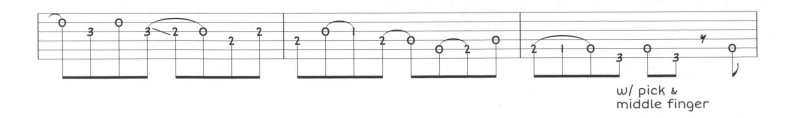

w/ pick &
middle finger

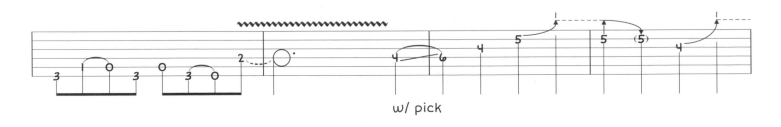

w/ pick

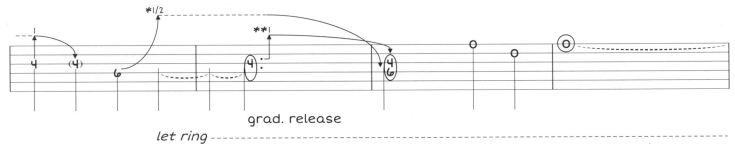

grad. release

let ring ---
*Bend towards ceiling.
**Bend towards floor.

80

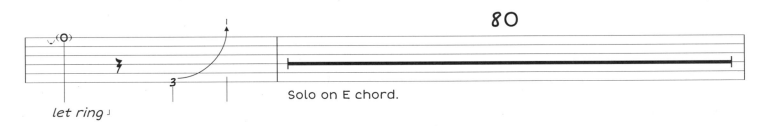

let ring ♩

Solo on E chord.

(1:55)

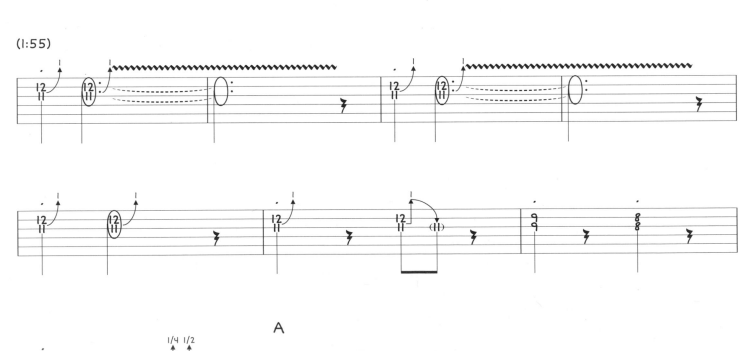

A

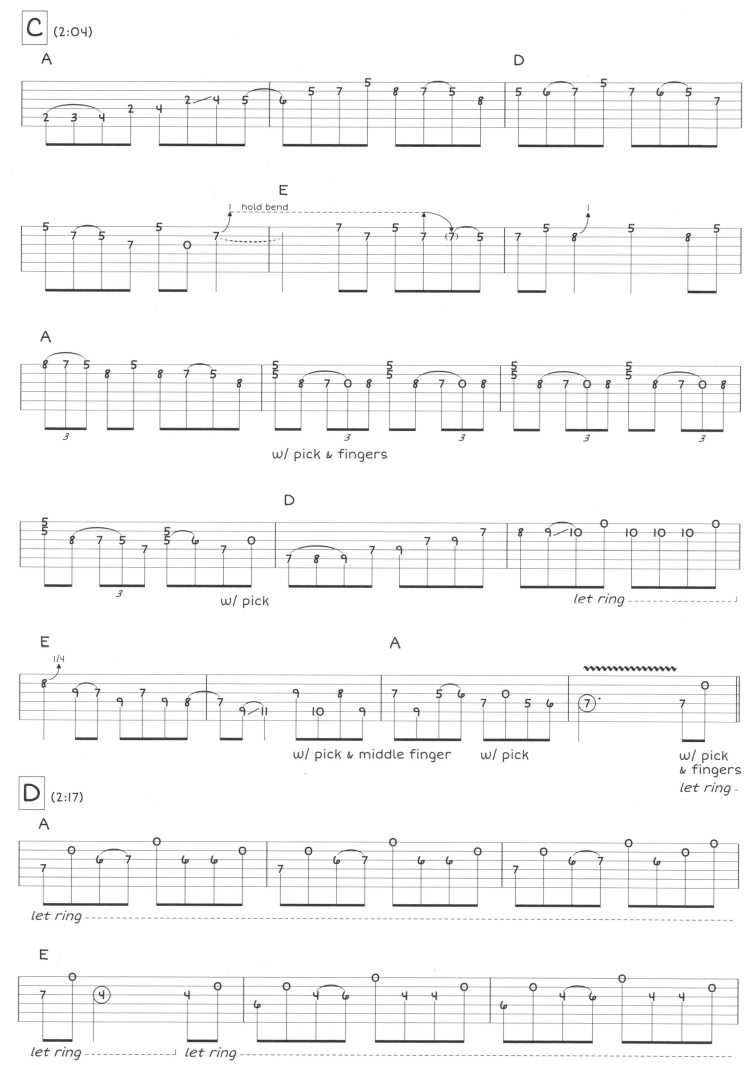

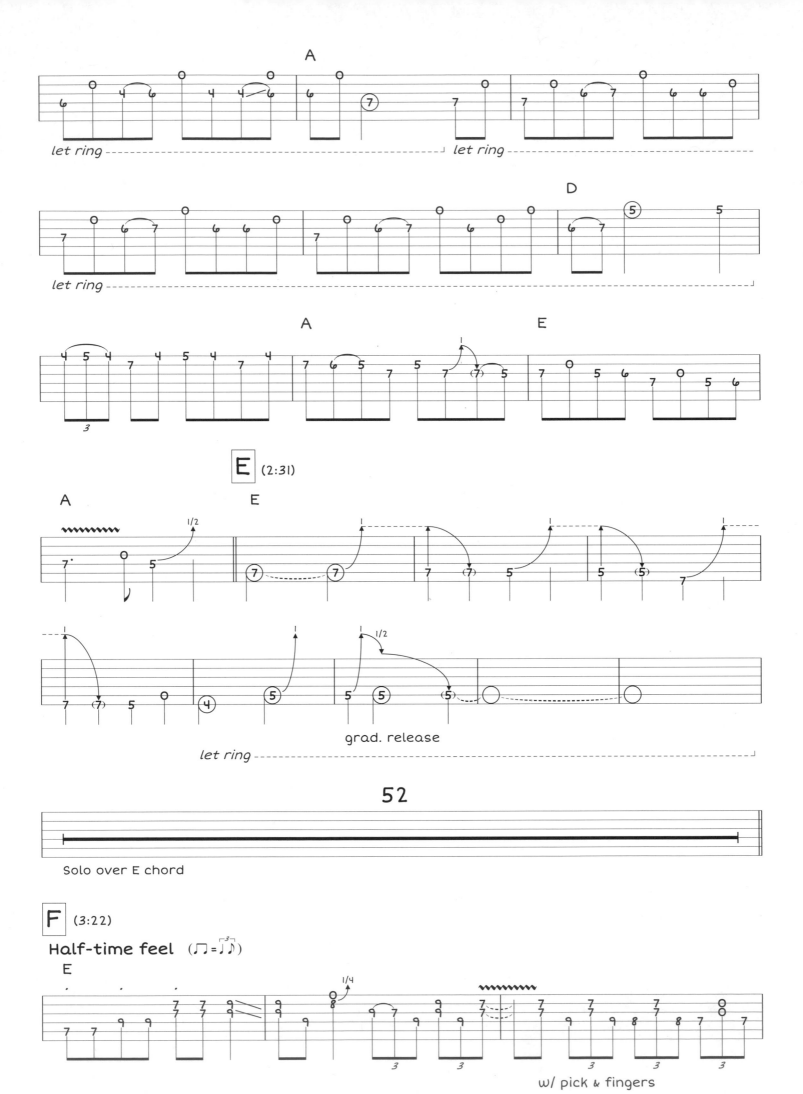

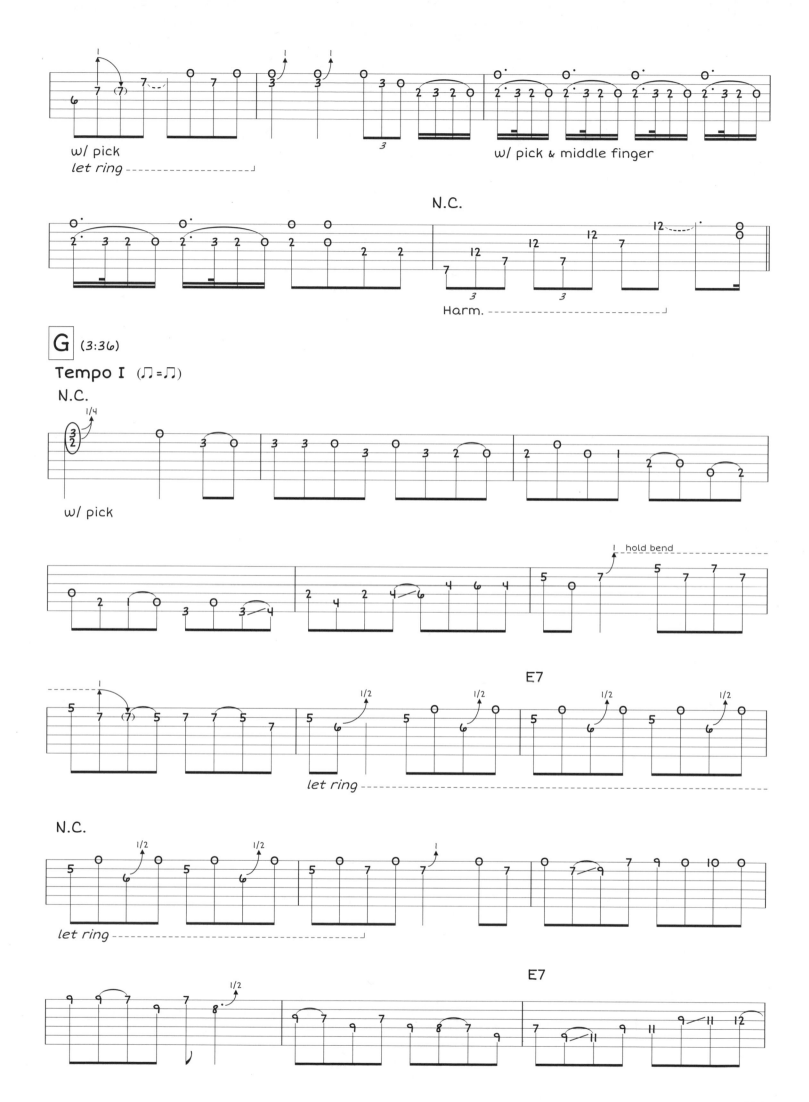

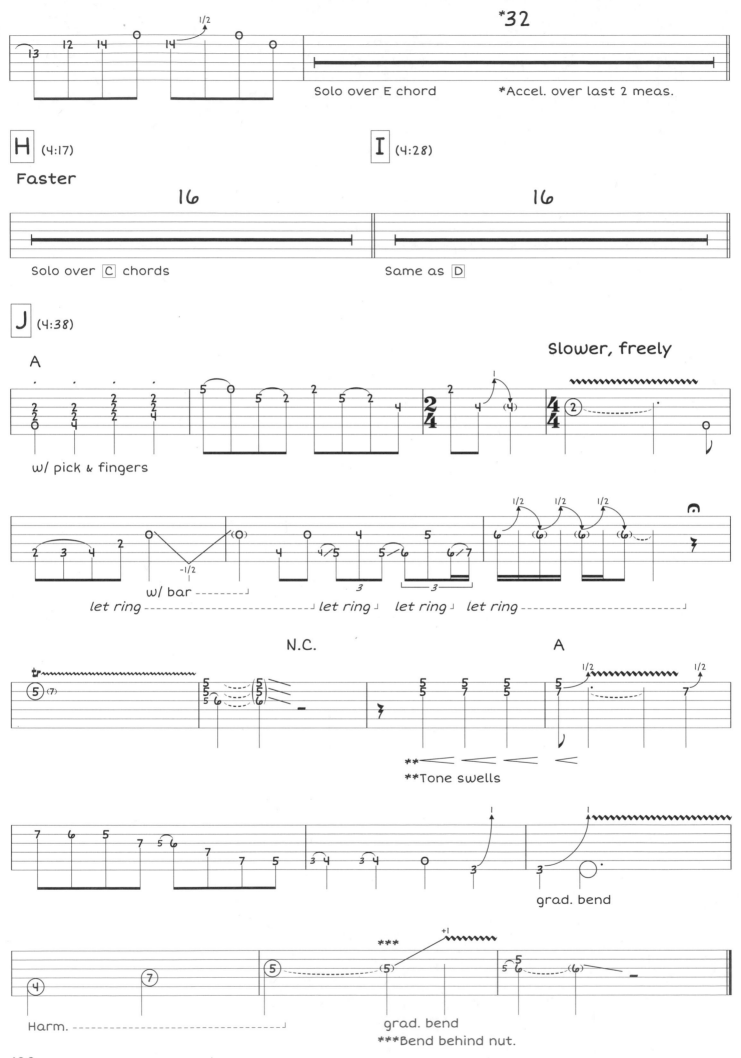

Restless

Words and Music by Carl Perkins

**Guitar: Ricky Scaggs,
Steve Wariner, Vince Gill**

Key of C
  Intro
   Very fast

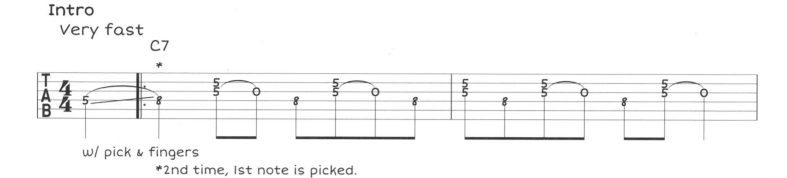

w/ pick & fingers
    *2nd time, 1st note is picked.

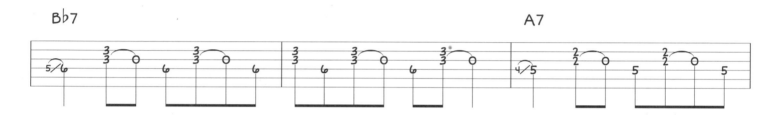

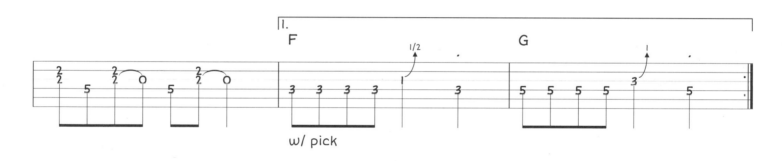

w/ pick

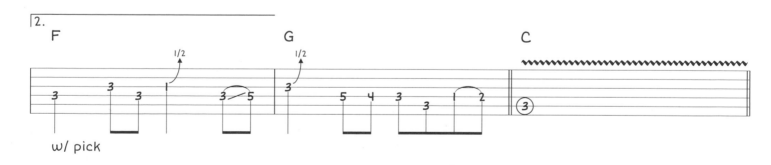

w/ pick

Verse

Well, I walked

|C |C |C |C |

|C |C |C |C   ‖

Chorus

'Cause I'm restless

F	F	F	F
C	C	C	C
D	D	G	G
C	F	C	G

Guitar Solo

C

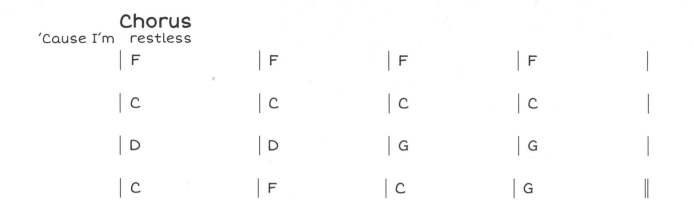

w/ pick & middle finger

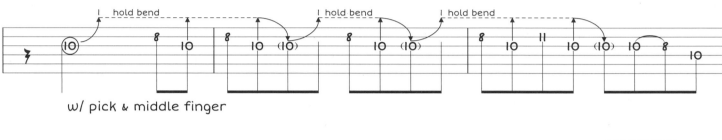

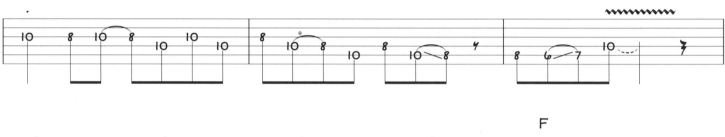

F

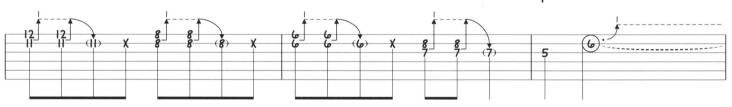

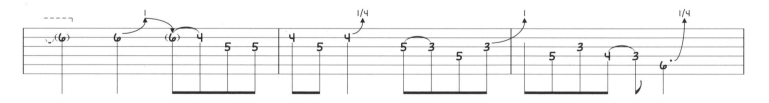

C

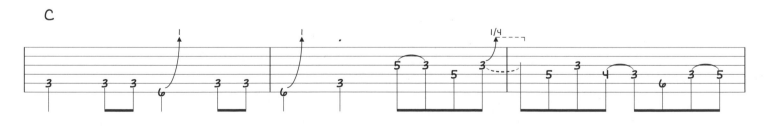

D

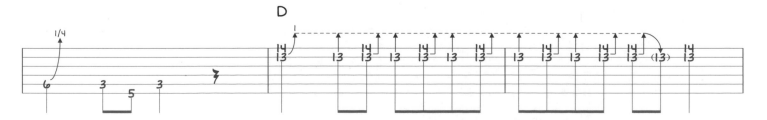

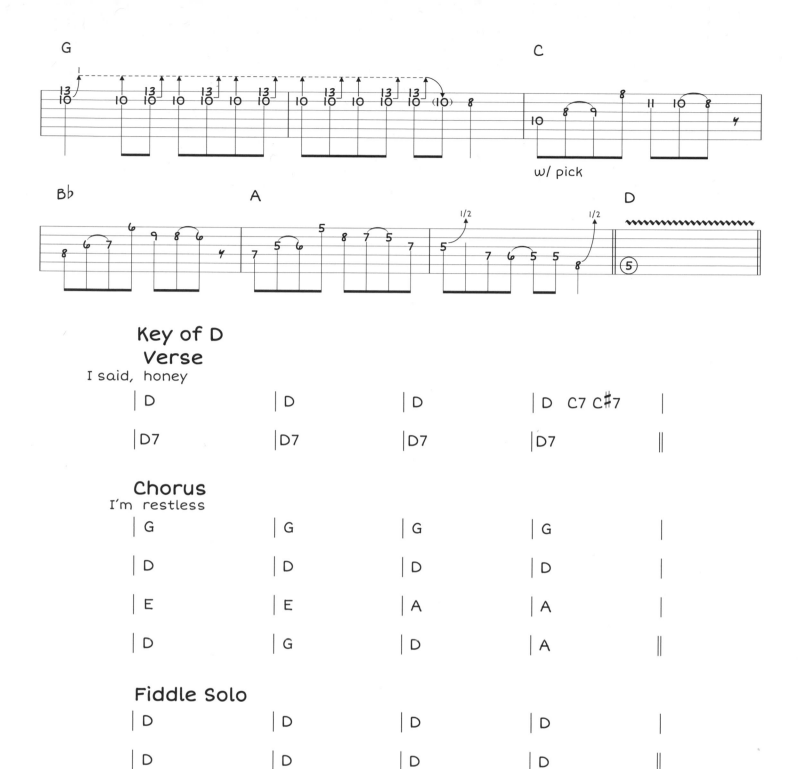

Key of D
Verse
I said, honey

| D | D | D | D C7 C#7 |
| D7 | D7 | D7 | D7 |

Chorus
I'm restless

G	G	G	G
D	D	D	D
E	E	A	A
D	G	D	A

Fiddle Solo

| D | D | D | D |
| D | D | D | D |

Guitar Solo

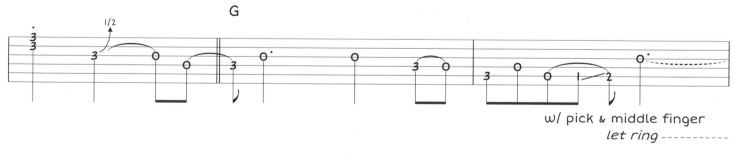

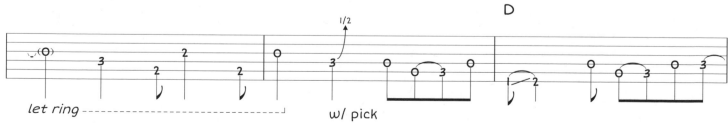

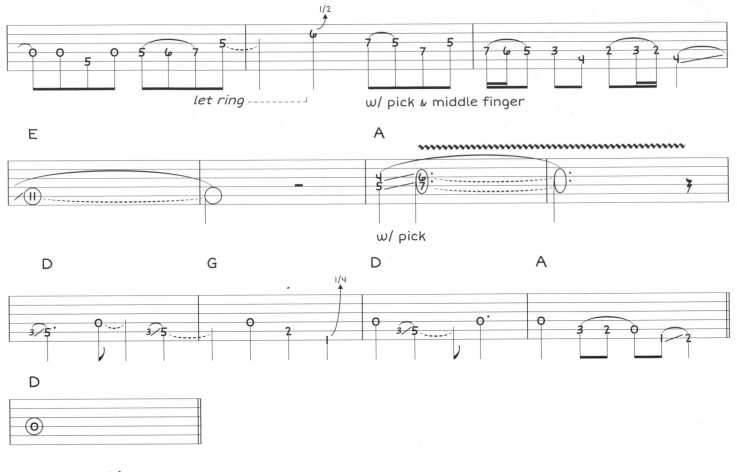

Verse

I'm travelin' light

|D |D |D |D |

|D |D |D |D   ‖

Chorus

'Cause I'm restless

|G |G |G |G |

|D |D |D |D |

|E |E |A |A |

|D |C7 |B7 |B7 |

|E   D/F# |G   E/G# |A   G/B |C   A/C# |

|D |G |D |A   ‖

Guitar Solo

D

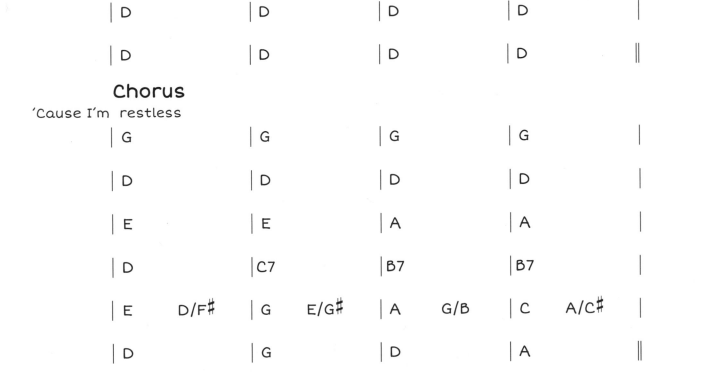

w/ pick & fingers

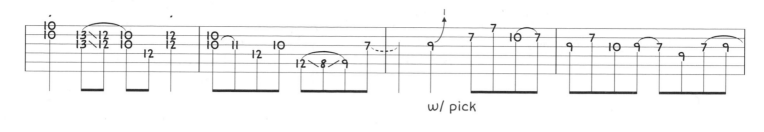

G

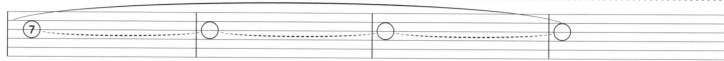

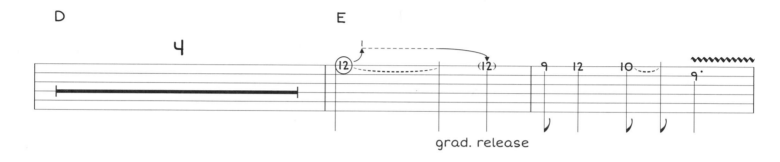

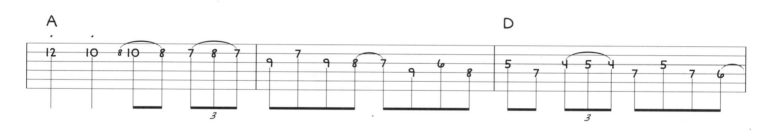

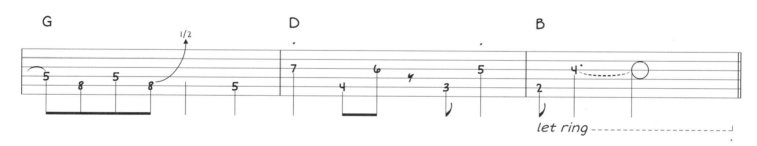

Key of E
Outro-Solos

E	E	E	E	
E	E	E	E	
A	A	A	A	
E	E	E	E	
F#	F#	B	B	
E	A	E	B	

127

Pride o' the Farm

By Steve Morse

Guitar: Steve Morse

Key of G

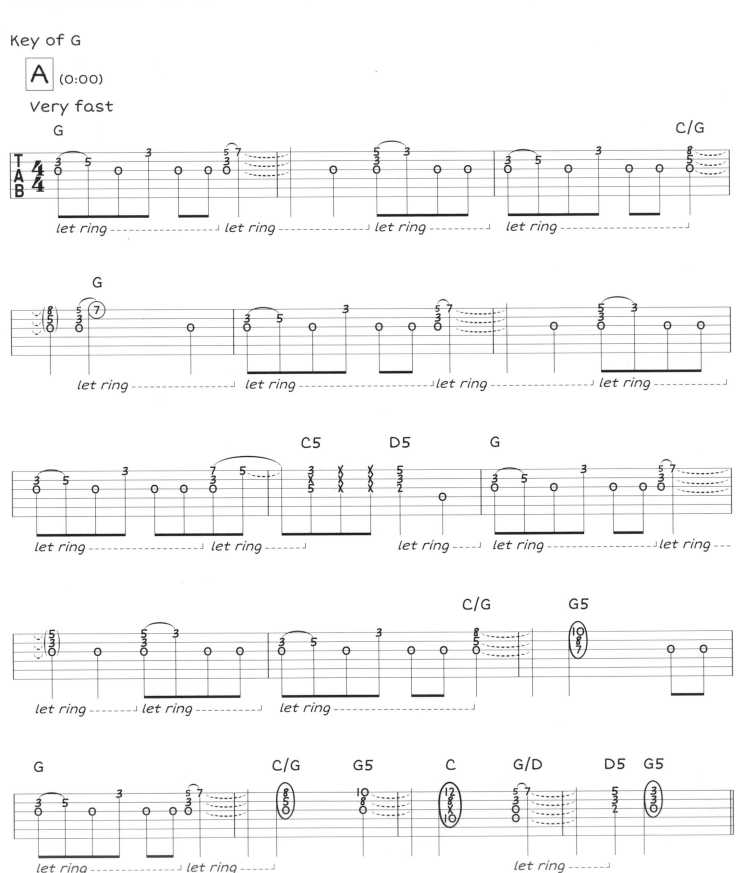

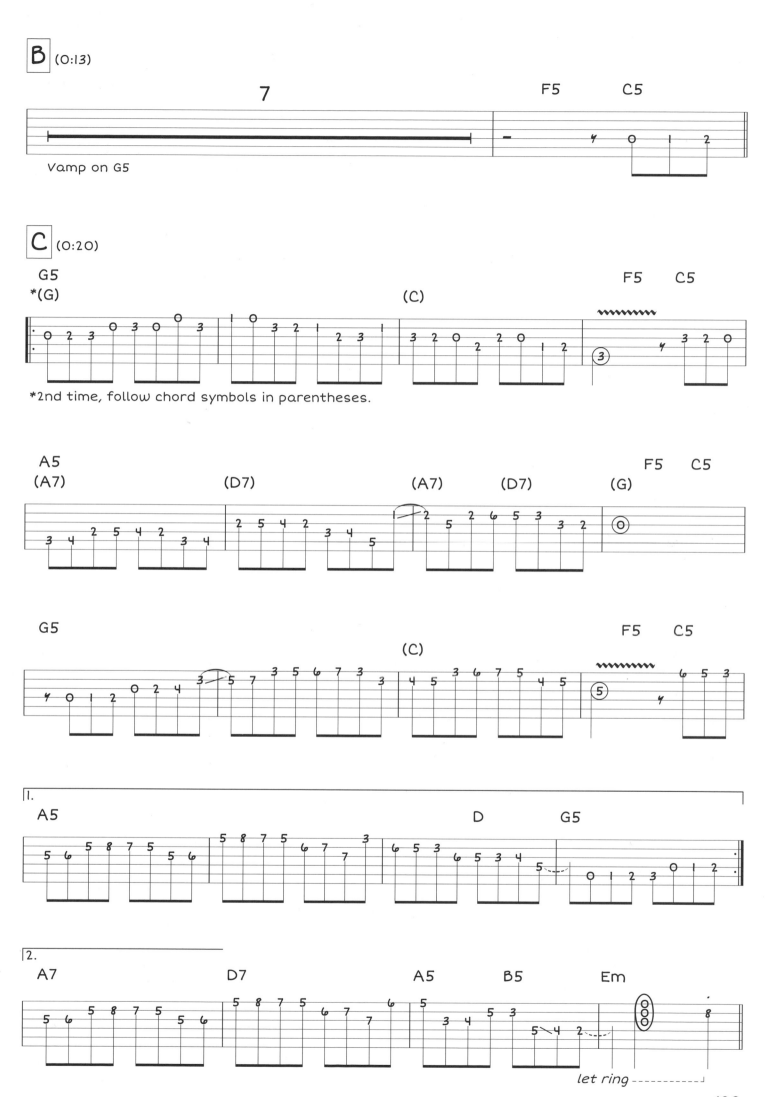

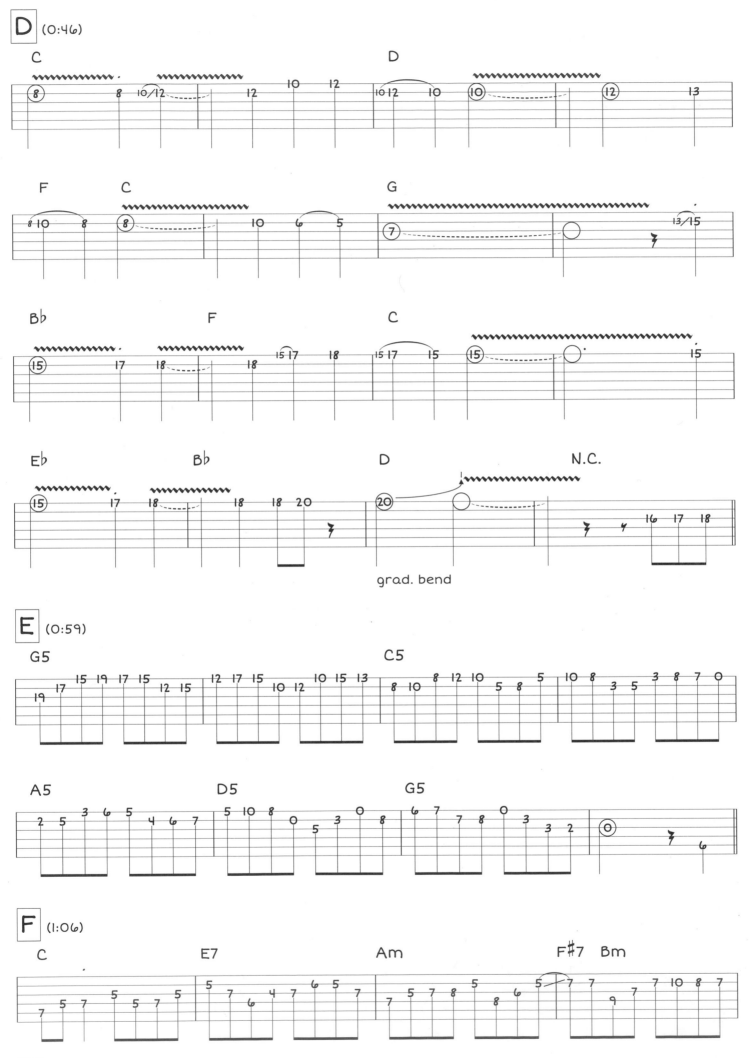

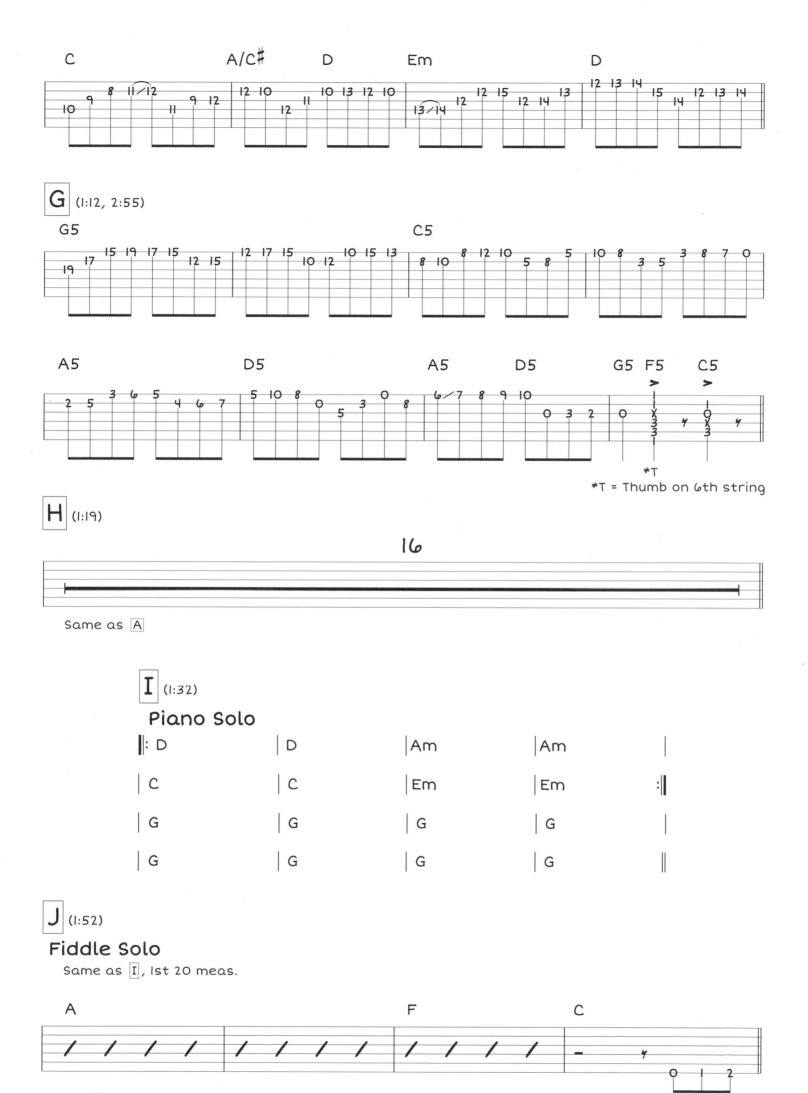

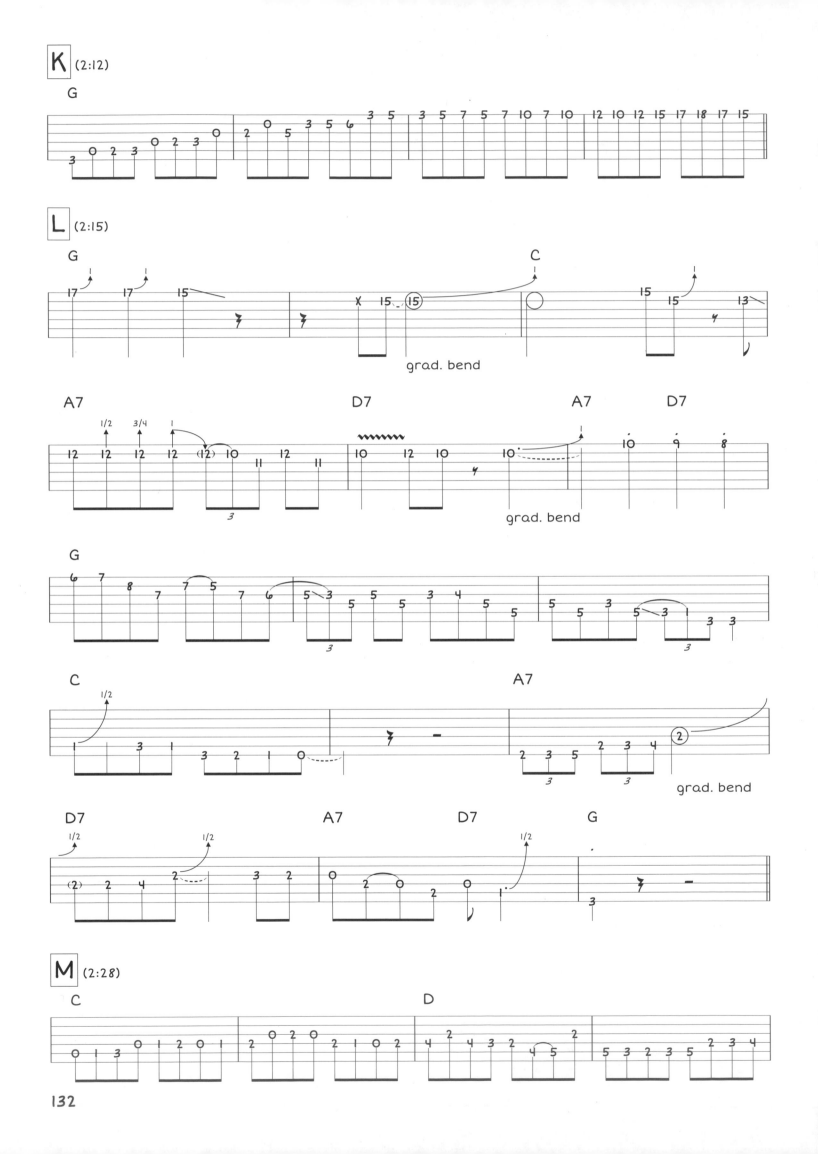

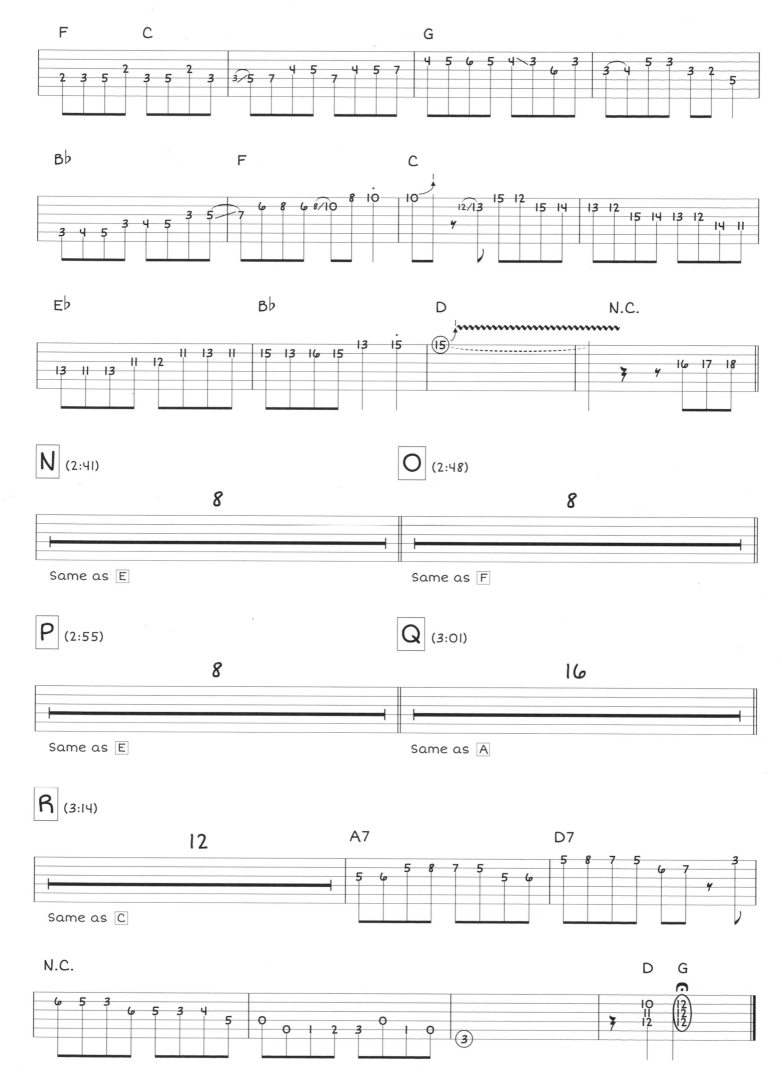

Red Hot Picker

By John Knowles

Guitar: Jerry Reed

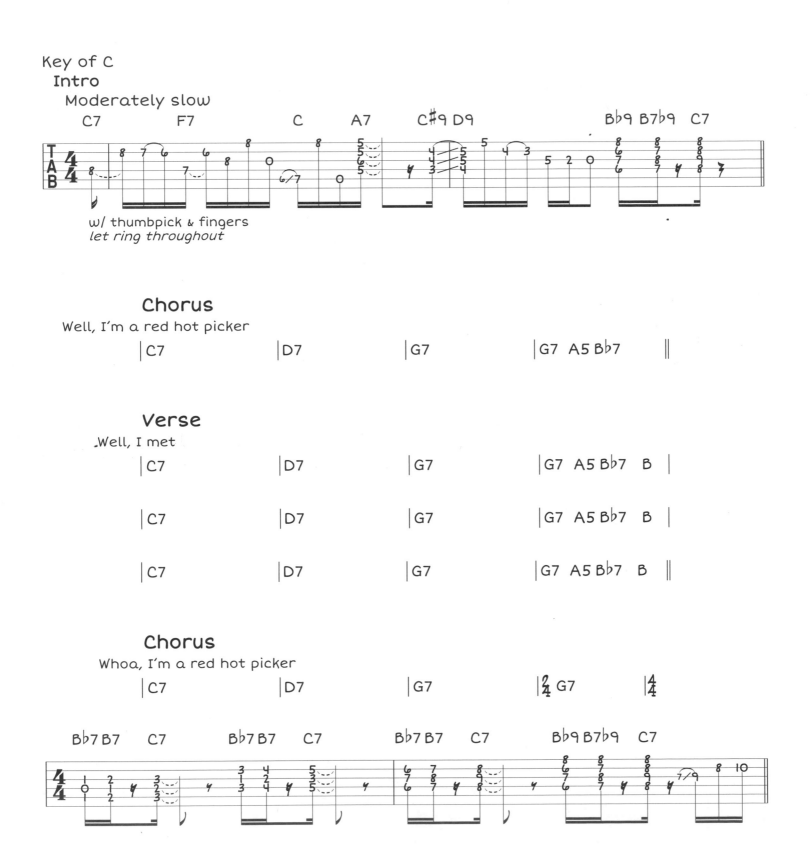

Interlude

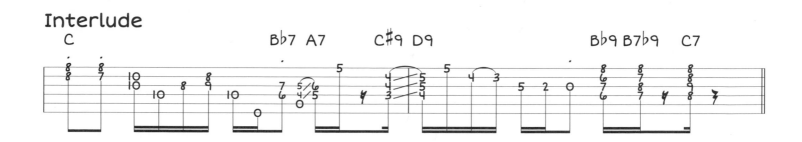

Guitar Solo

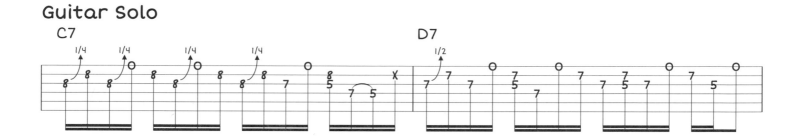

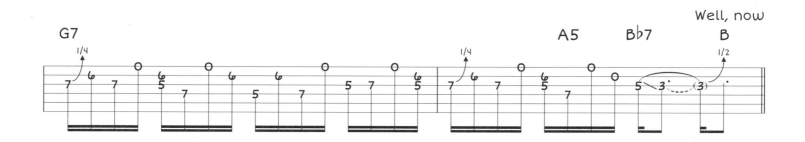

Verse

some time later

Ending

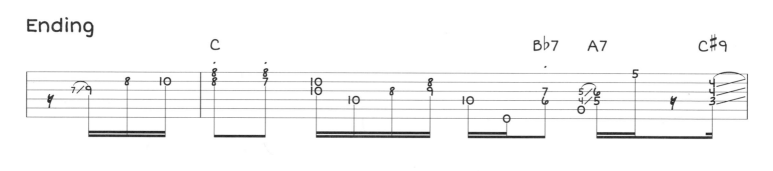

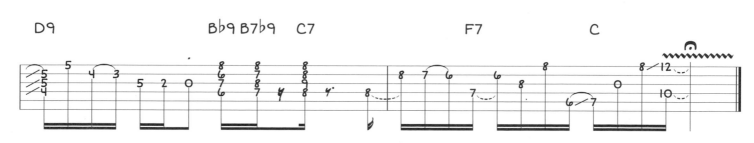

135

from Rodney Crowell - *Diamonds & Dirt*

She's Crazy for Leavin'
Words and Music by Guy Clark and Rodney Crowell

Guitar: Steuart Smith

Key of E
Intro
Very fast (♫ = ♩♪)

E

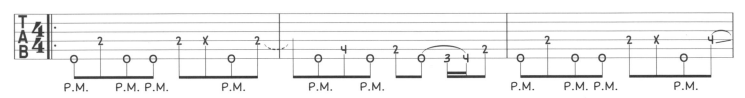

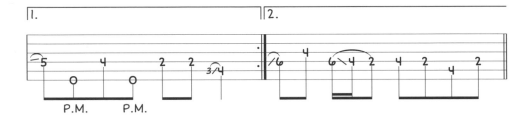

Verse
Well, the bus   pulled   away

E	E	A	A	
B	B	E	E	
E	E	A	A	
B	B	B	E	
E	‖			

Chorus
She's   crazy   for leavin'.

A	A	B	E	
E	E	B	B	
A	A	B	E	
A	E	B	‖	

Interlude
w/ Intro riff

E	E	E	E	‖

Guitar Solo

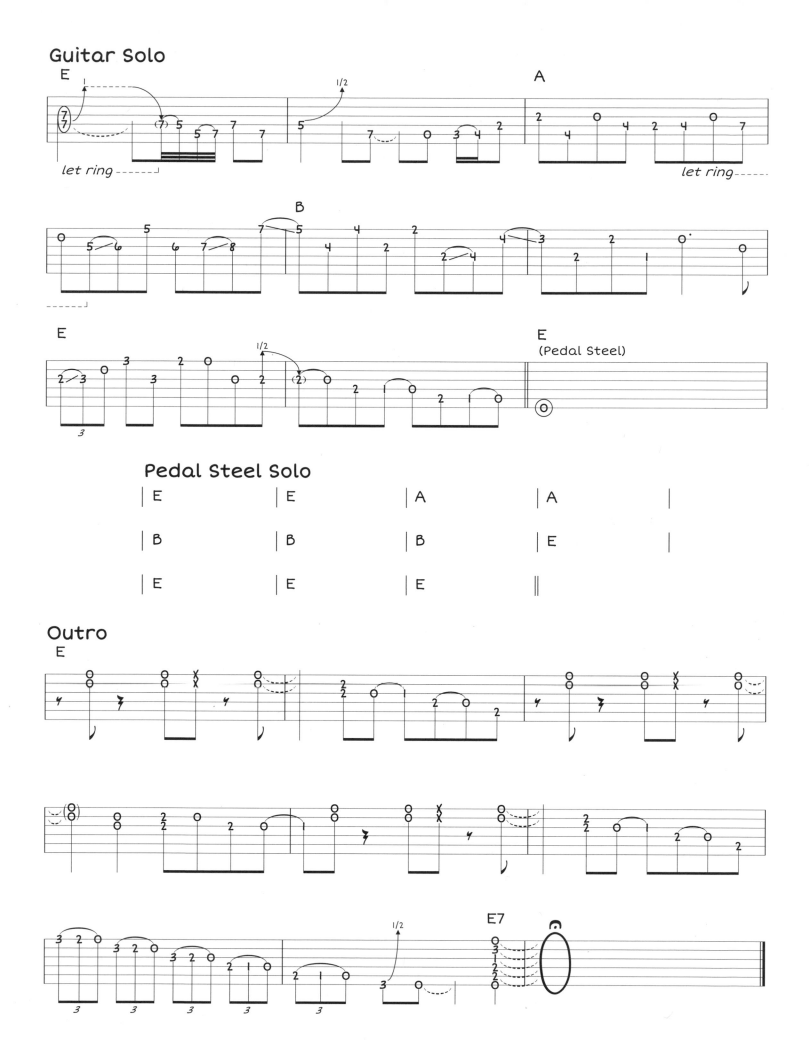

Pedal Steel Solo

Outro

from Bob Wills and His Texas Playboys - *The Essential Bob Wills 1935-1947*

Stay a Little Longer
(The Hoedown Fiddle Song)
Words and Music by Tommy Duncan

Guitar: Eldon Shamblin

Key of G

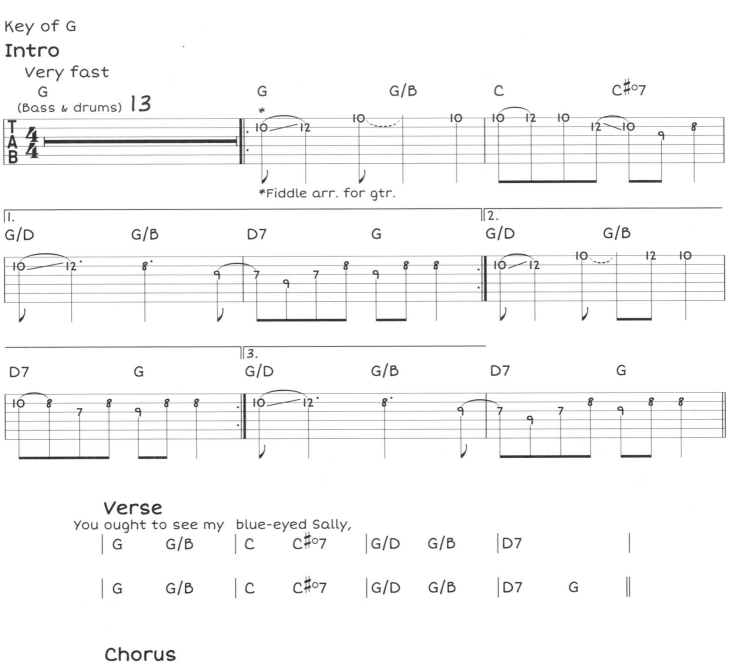

Verse

You ought to see my blue-eyed Sally,

| G | G/B | C | C#°7 | G/D | G/B | D7 | |

| G | G/B | C | C#°7 | G/D | G/B | D7 | G |

Chorus

Stay all night, stay a little longer.

| G | | G | D7 | D7 | |

| G | | C | G | 2/4 D7 | 4/4 |

| 4/4 G | | |

Solos

G G/B	C C#°7	G/D G/B	D7
G G/B	C C#°7	G/D G/B	D7 G
G G/B	C C#°7	G/D G/B	D7
G G/B	C C#°7	G/D G/B	D7 G	

Guitar Solo

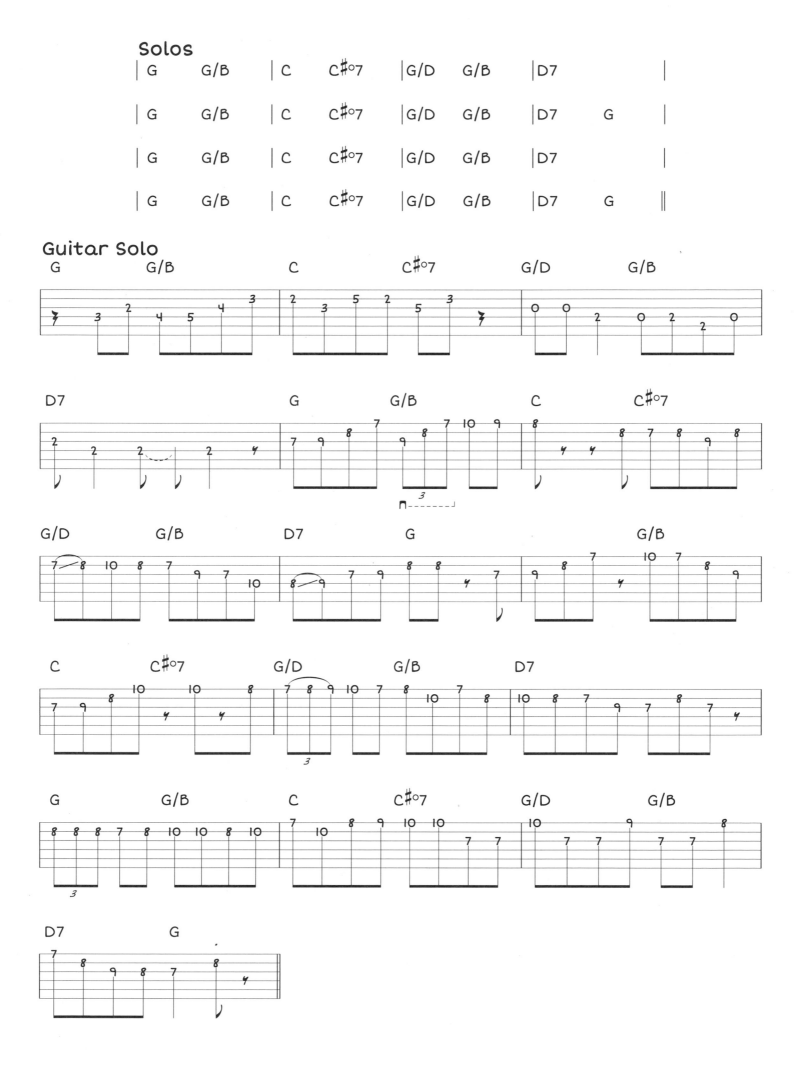

Sugarfoot Rag

Words and Music by Hank Garland and Vaughn Horton

Guitar: Hank Garland

Key of A

Intro　　　　　　　　　　　　　　　　　　　　　　　**Head**

Moderately, in 2

Fiddle Solos

```
|A          |G          |A          |E     A     |
|A          |G          |A          |E     A     |
|A          |A          |A          |E     A     |
|A      ·   |A          |A          |E     A     ‖
```

Guitar Solo

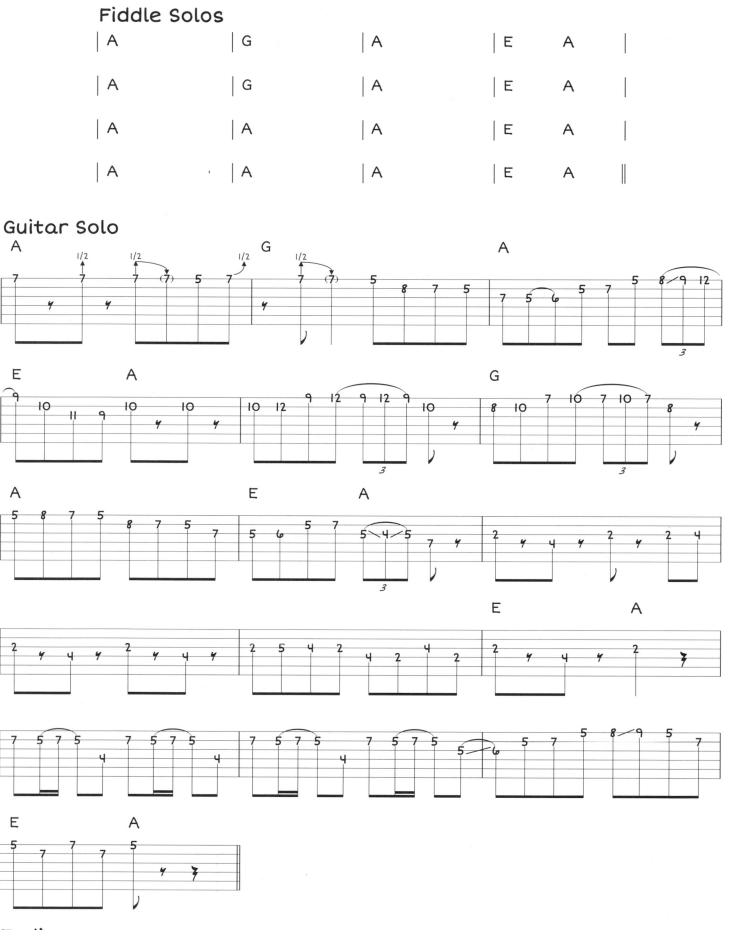

Ending

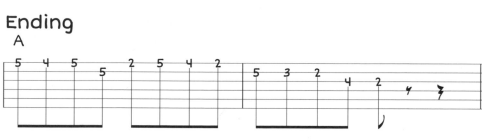

from Clint Black - *One Emotion*

Summer's Comin'

Words and Music by Clint Black and Nicholas Hayden

Guitar: Dan Huff

Key of A
Intro
Fast
N.C.

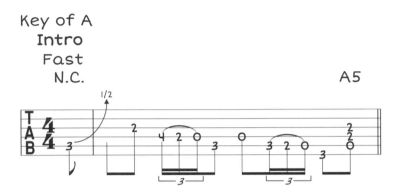

Chorus
Nothin' on Earth

	A5		A5		A5		A5	
	D5		D5		D5		D5	
	A5		A5		A5		A5	
	E5		E5		A5		A5	‖

Verse
I'm taking off

	E5		E5		D5		A5	
	E5		E5		G5		D5	
	A5		E5		E5	‖	

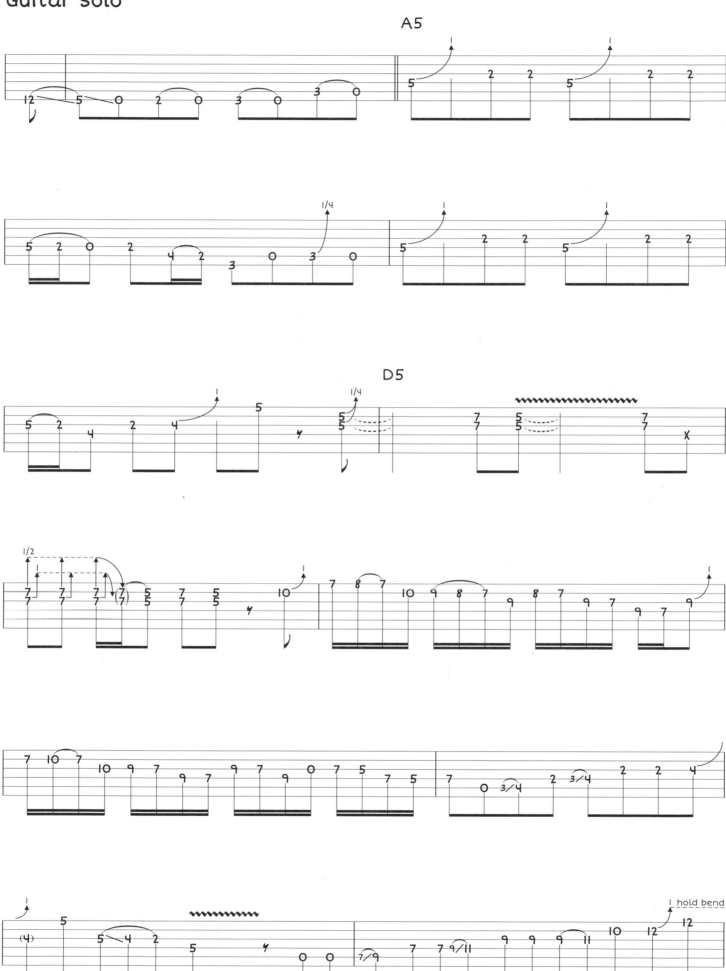

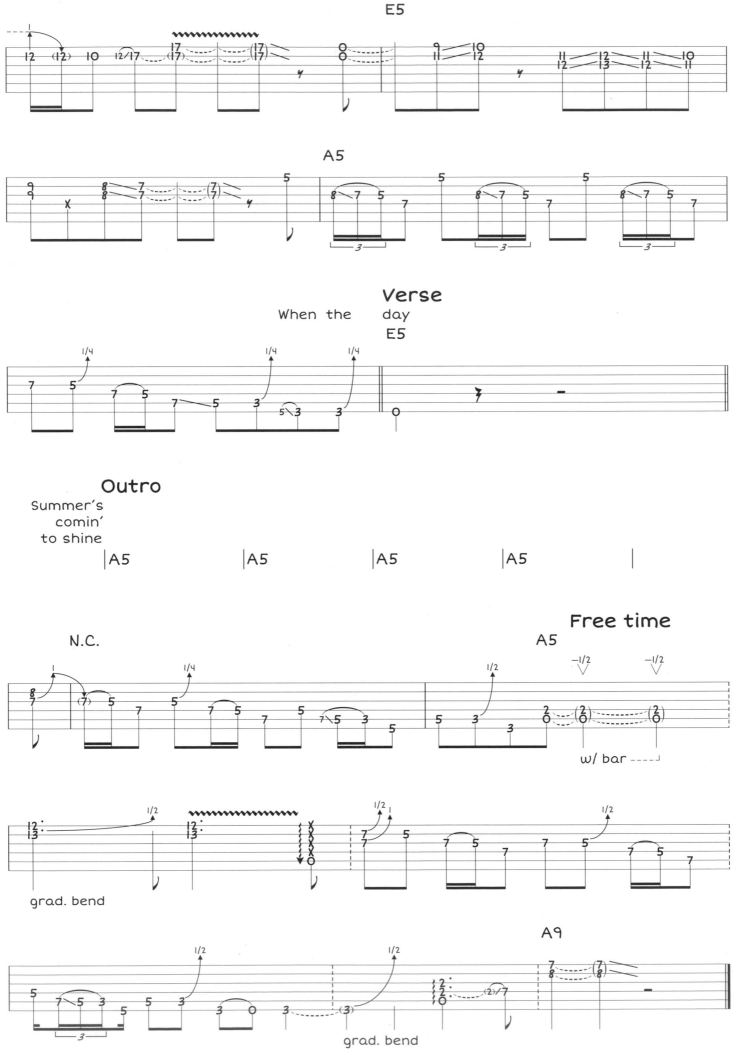

Verse

When the   day

Outro

Summer's
comin'
to shine

Free time

w/ bar

grad. bend

grad. bend

Sweet Little Lisa

Words and Music by Donivan Cowart, Hank DeVito and Walter Cowart

Guitar: Albert Lee

Key of A
  Intro
    Fast

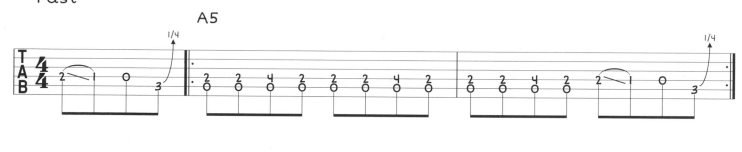

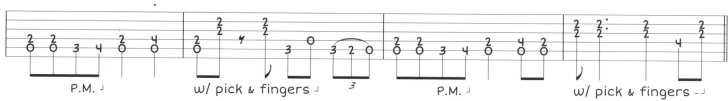

P.M.   w/ pick & fingers   P.M.   w/ pick & fingers

Verse
Well, the work whistle blew

	A5		A5		A5		A5	
	A5		A5		D5		D5	
	E5		E5		E5		E5	
	E5		E5		A5		A5	‖

Chorus
'Cause there ain't nobody

	D5		D5		A5		A5	
	E5		E5		E5		A5	
	D5		D5		A5		A5	
	E5		E5		E5		A5	‖

Interlude

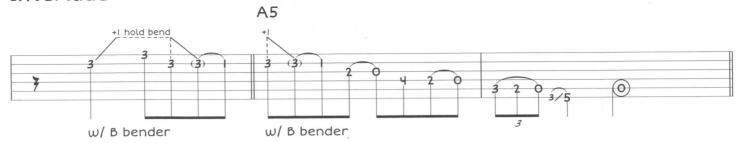

w/ B bender   w/ B bender

Chorus

'Cause there ain't nobody

	D5		D5		A5		A5	
	E5		E5		E5		A5	
	D5		D5		A5		A5	
	E5		E5		E5	‖	

Interlude

w/ Intro riff

	A5		A5		A5		A5	‖

Guitar Solo

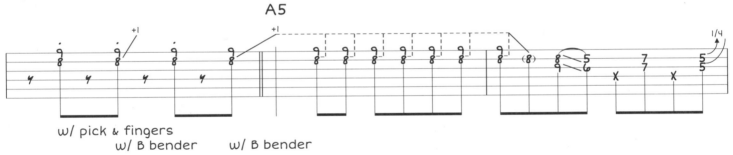

w/ pick & fingers
w/ B bender   w/ B bender

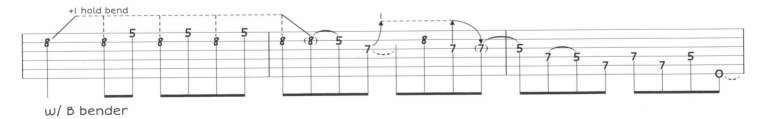

w/ B bender

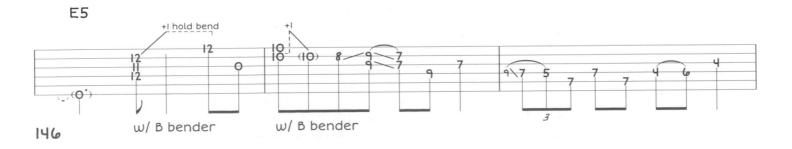

146   w/ B bender   w/ B bender

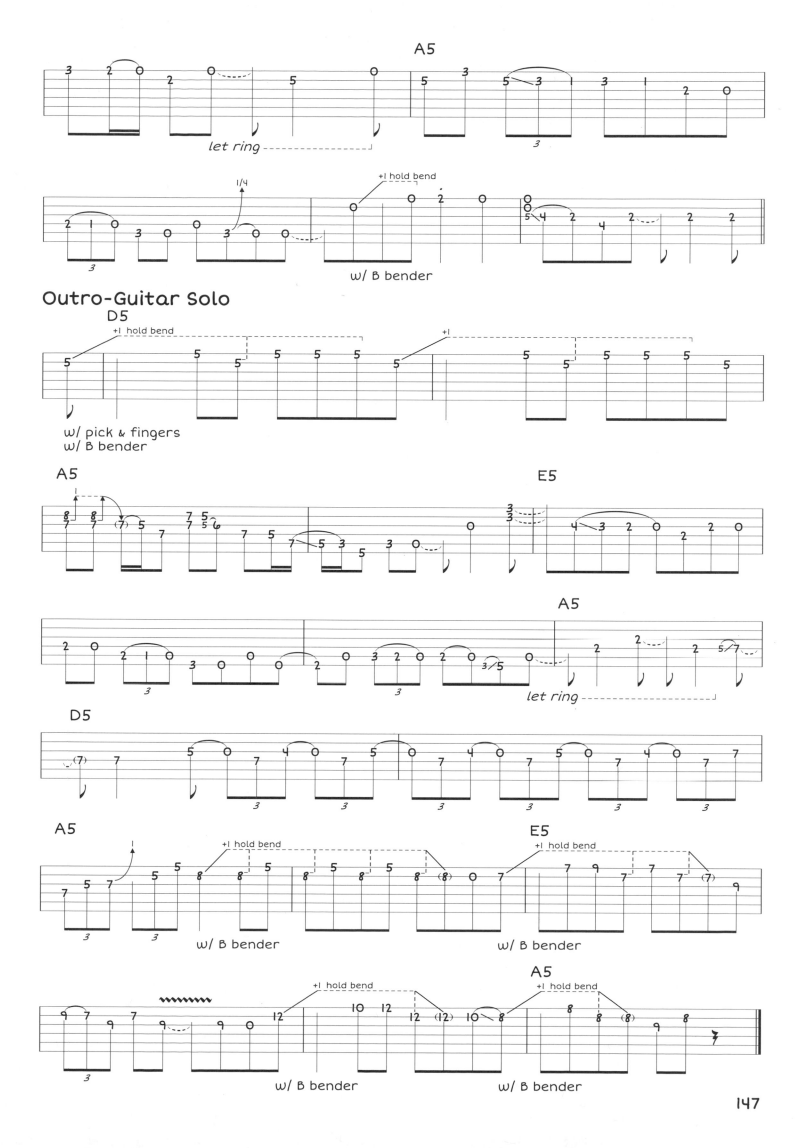

Outro-Guitar Solo

Tennessee Whiskey

Words and Music by Dean Dillon and Linda Hargrove

Guitar: Chris Stapleton

Key of A

Intro

Slow, in 4

w/ slight dist.

Verse

Used to spend my nights out in barrooms.

A	|Bm	
|Bm	|A D/A A	
	A	|Bm	
	Bm		A D/A A ‖

Chorus

You're as smooth   as Tennessee whiskey.

A D/A A	|Bm	
|Bm	|A D/A A	
	A	|Bm	
	Bm		A D/A A ‖

Guitar Solo

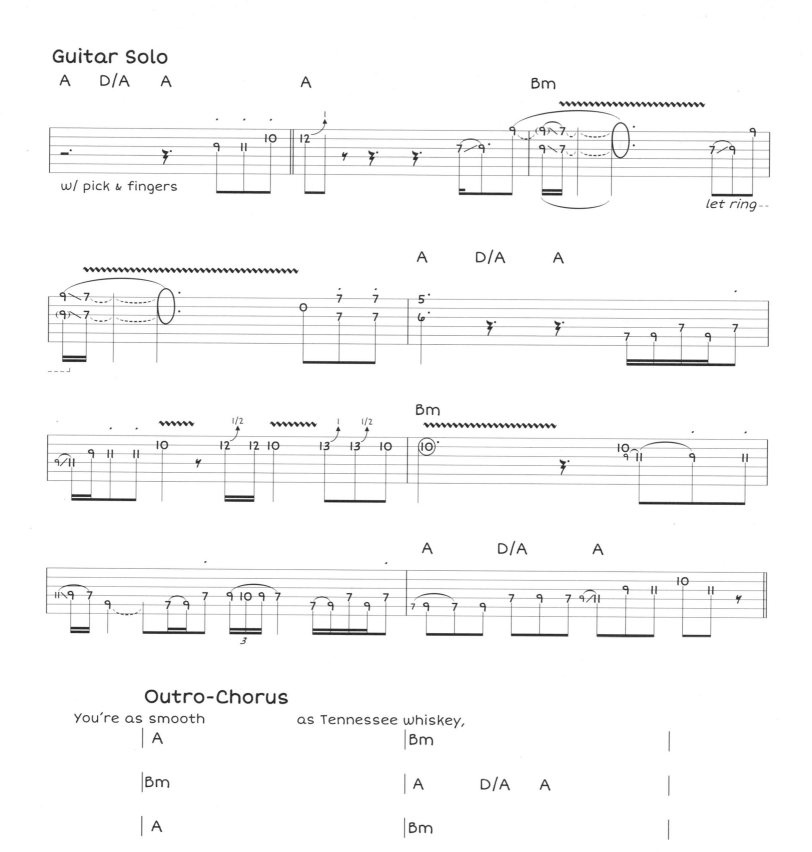

w/ pick & fingers

let ring--

Outro-Chorus

You're as smooth   as Tennessee whiskey,

A		Bm	
|Bm	|A D/A A	
|A	|Bm	
|Bm	|A	

That's What I Like About You

Words and Music by John Hadley, Kevin Welch and Wally Wilson

Guitar: Brent Mason

Tune down 1/2 step:
(low to high) E♭-A♭-D♭-G♭-B♭-E♭

Key of E

Intro

Moderately, in 2

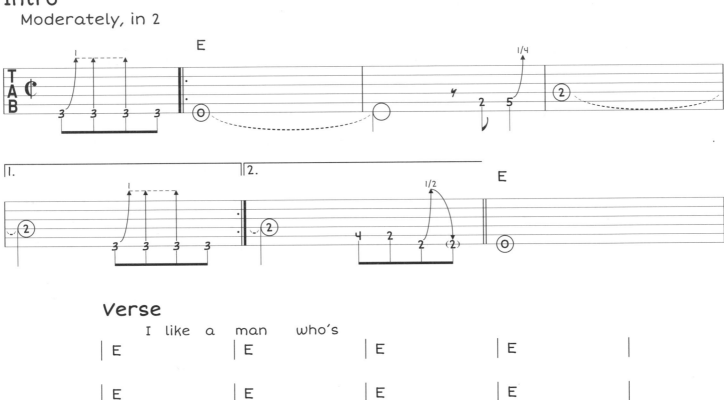

Verse

I like a man who's

E	E	E	E
E	E	E	E
A7	A7	B7	B7
E	E	E	E

Bridge

Don't want a man to be

B7	B7	B7	B7 A
E	E A	E	E
B7	B7	B7	B7
A7	A7	A7	B7
B7   A

Guitar Solo

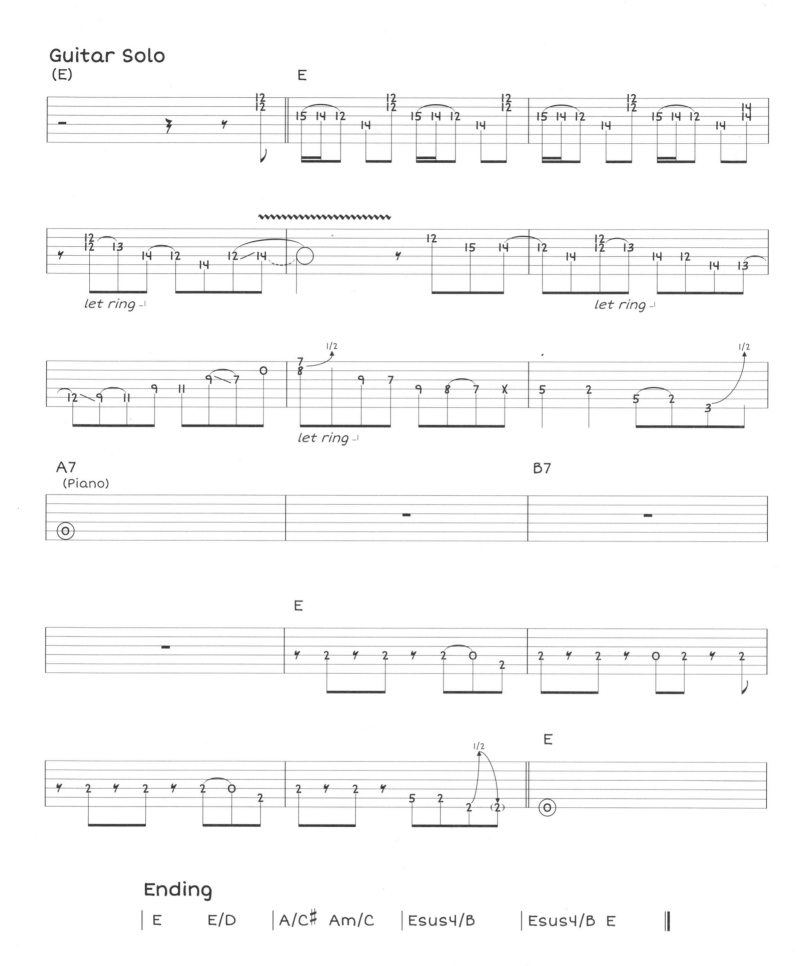

Ending

| E   E/D |A/C# Am/C |Esus4/B |Esus4/B E   ‖

Uncle Pen
Words and Music by Bill Monroe

Guitar: Ray Flacke

Key of A
  Intro
   Very fast
   N.C.

4/4 A	A	A A/C#	E A
A	A	A A/C#	E A
D	A	A A/C#	E A
A	A	A A/C#	2/4 E	4/4

| 4/4 A | A | ‖ |

Verse
Oh, the people

A	A	A A/C#	E A
A	A	A A/C#	2/4 E	4/4

| 4/4 A | A | ‖ |

Chorus
Late in the evening

D	A	A A/C#	E A
A N.C.		A N.C.	2/4	4/4

w/ Intro riff

| 4/4 | 2/4 | ‖ 4/4 |

Interlude

4/4 A	A	A A/C#	E A
A	A	A A/C#	E A ‖

Pedal Steel Solo

D	A	A A/C#	E A
A	A	A A/C# 2/4 E	4/4
4/4 A	A	

Guitar Solo

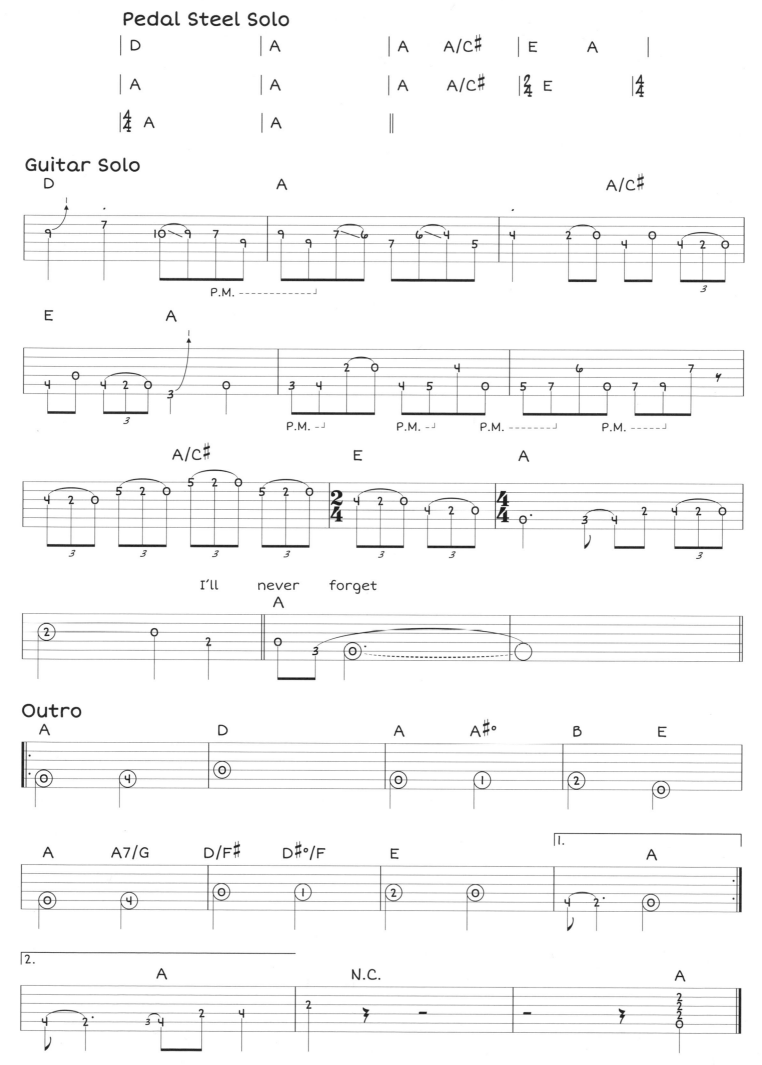

I'll never forget

Outro

153

from Tracy Byrd - *No Ordinary Man*

Watermelon Crawl

Words and Music by Buddy Brock and Zack Turner

Guitar: Brent Mason

Key of G
Intro
Moderately fast
N.C.

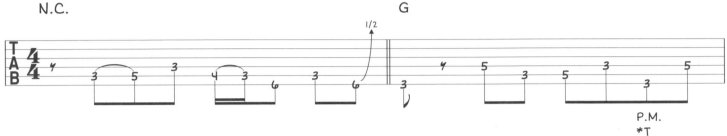

*T = Thumb on 6th string

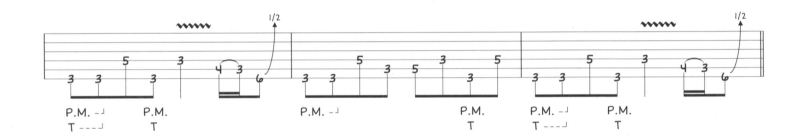

Verse
I was driving

| | G | | G | | G | | D | G | |

| | G | | C | | G | | $\frac{2}{4}$ D | | $\frac{4}{4}$ |

Interlude
w/ Intro riff

| $\frac{4}{4}$ G | | G | ‖

Chorus
He said,
"We've got..."

| | C | | C | | G | | G | |

| | C | | C | | G N.C. | | D N.C. | ‖

Interlude

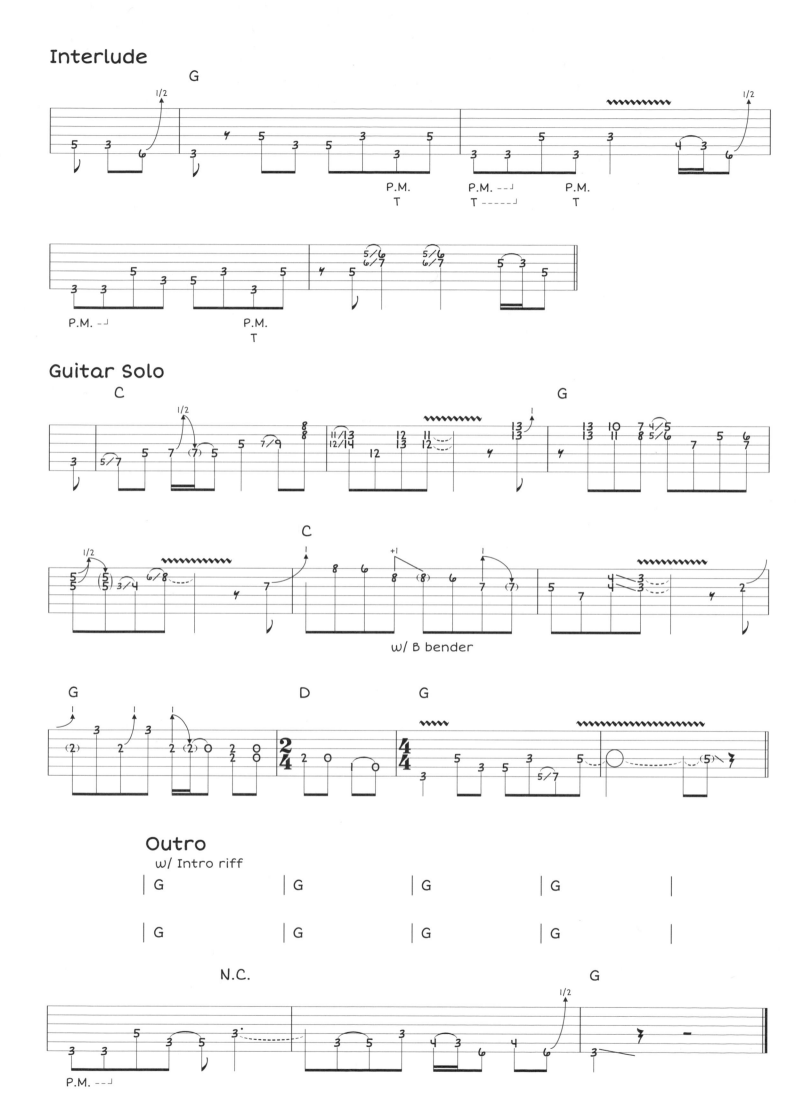

Guitar Solo

Outro

w/ Intro riff

from Brooks & Dunn - *Waitin' on Sundown*

Whiskey Under the Bridge

Words and Music by Kix Brooks, Ronnie Dunn and Don Cook

Guitar: Brent Mason

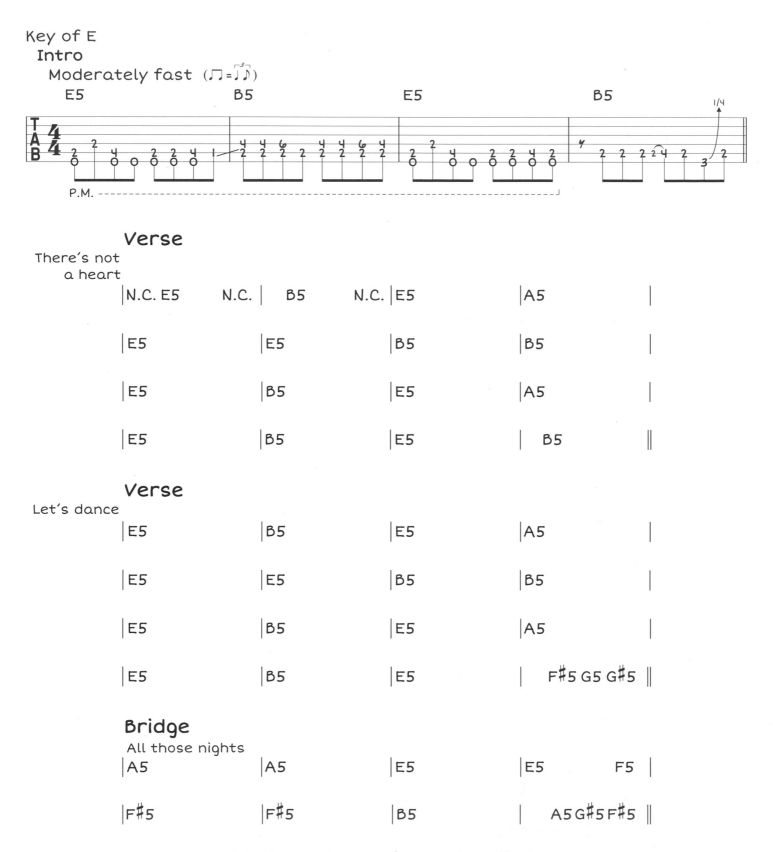

Guitar Solo

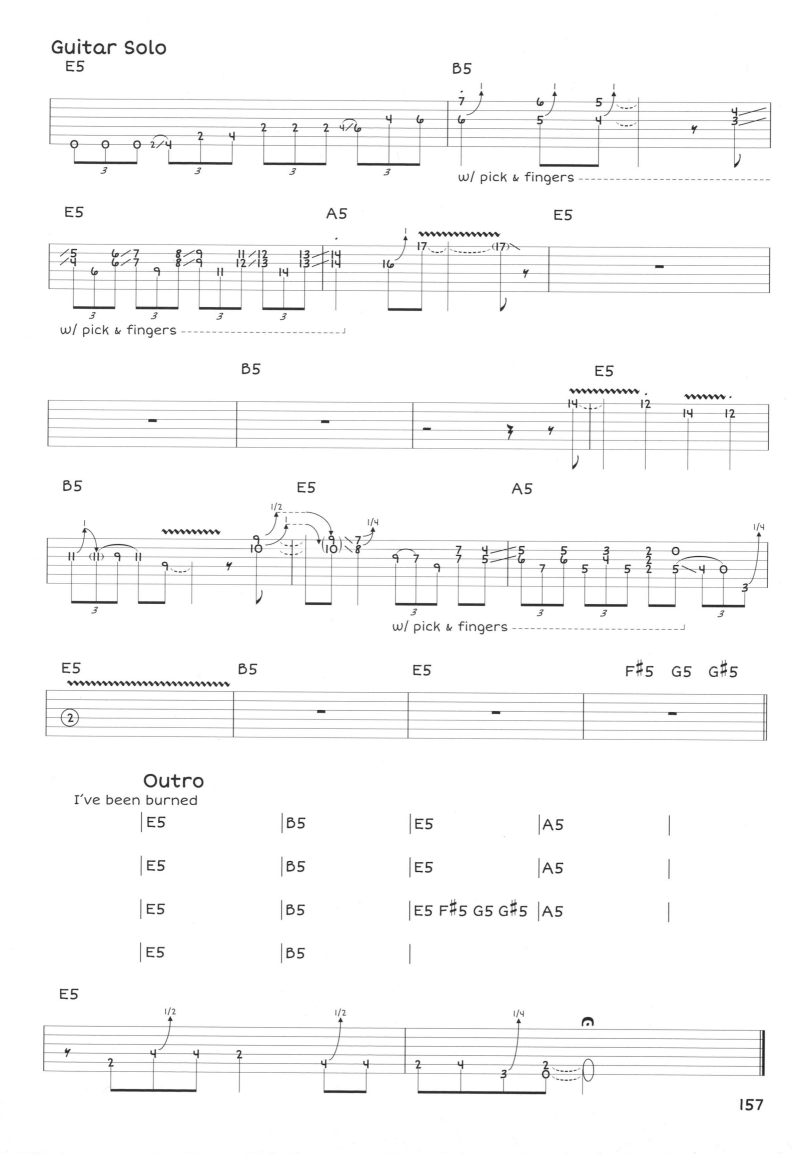

Outro
I've been burned

|E5 |B5 |E5 |A5 |

|E5 |B5 |E5 |A5 |

|E5 |B5 |E5 F#5 G5 G#5 |A5 |

|E5 |B5 | |

E5

from Dixie Chicks - *Fly*

Some Days You Gotta Dance

Words and Music by Troy Johnson and Marshall Morgan

Guitar: Keith Urban

Key of E
Intro
Fast

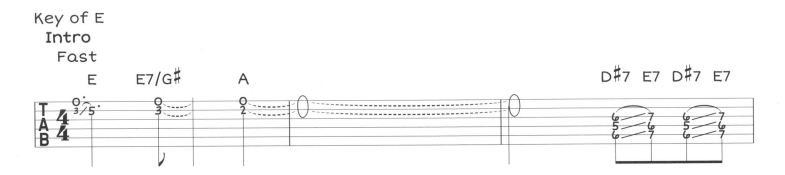

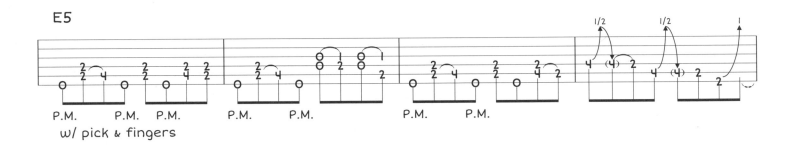

w/ pick & fingers

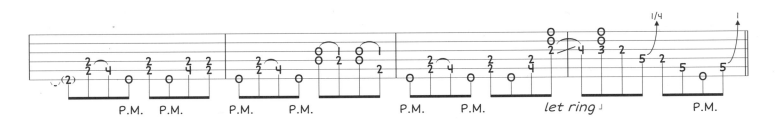

Verse

It was about five

	E5		E5		E5		E5	
	E5		E5		E5		E5	
	A5		A5		E5		E5	
	B5		B5		*B N.C.		

*2nd time: B7#9

Chorus

Some days

|E5 |E5 |E5 |E5 |

|A5 |A5 |E5 |E5 |

|B5 |A5   ‖

Interlude

|E5 | D♯7 E7 D♯7 E7 |E5 |E5   ‖

Chorus

|E5 |E5 |E5 |E5 |

|A5 |A5 |E5 |E5 |

|B5 |A5 |E5 |E5   ‖

Interlude

|E5 |E5 |E5 |

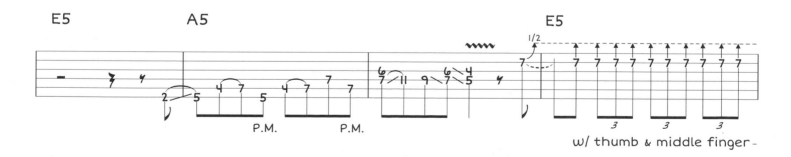

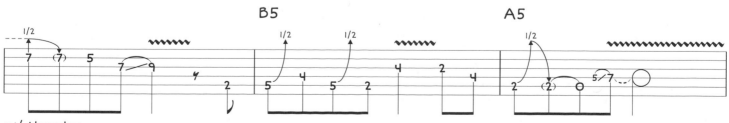

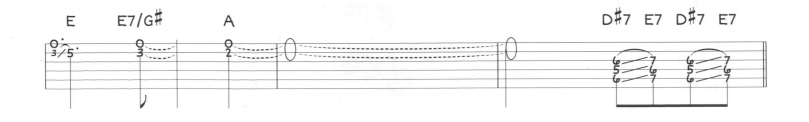

Outro-Chorus

Some days

N.C.

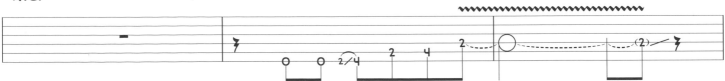

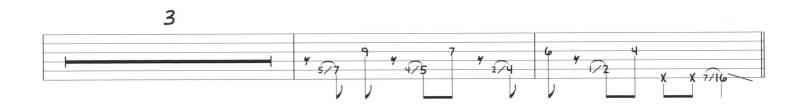

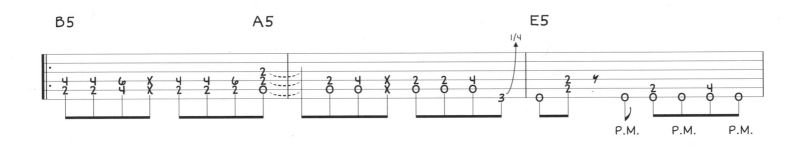

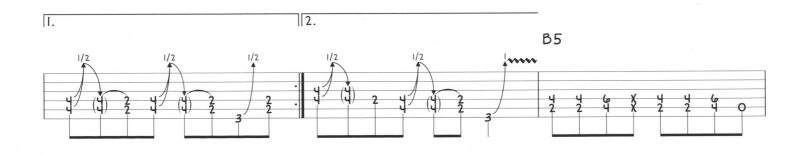

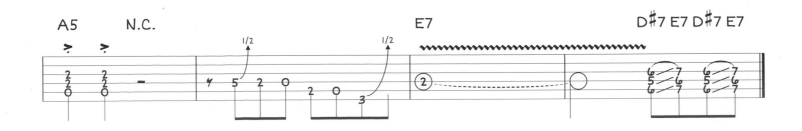